GLOBAL ISSUES IN A CHANGING WORLD

This new series of short, accessible think-pieces deals with leading global issues of relevance to humanity today. Intended for the enquiring reader and social activists in the North and the South, as well as students, the books explain what is at stake and question conventional ideas and policies. Drawn from many different parts of the world, the series' authors pay particular attention to the needs and interests of ordinary people, whether living in the rich industrial or the developing countries. They all share a common objective – to help stimulate new thinking and social action in the opening years of the new century.

Global Issues in a Changing World is a joint initiative by Zed Books in collaboration with a number of partner publishers and non-governmental organizations around the world. By working together, we intend to maximize the relevance and availability of the books published in the series.

PARTICIPATING NGOs

Both ENDS, Amsterdam
Catholic Institute for International Relations, London
Corner House, Sturminster Newton
Council on International and Public Affairs, New York
Dag Hammarskjöld Foundation, Uppsala
Development GAP, Washington DC

ngkok

, Delhi

ng

Accra

World Development Movement, London

CRITICAL PRAISE FOR THIS BOOK

Peter Robbins presents a comprehensive picture of the fall in global commodity prices, its impact on global poverty and of the factors underlying this crisis. In itself this is an important contribution to knowledge. But much more important is his reminder that this crisis in prices and incomes arises from the workings of a market system with a growing asymmetry of power – global buyers grow ever larger and more powerful, whereas commodity producers have been fragmented as the international agencies have systematically undermined marketing boards, governments in poor countries and agreements between poor countries to bolster prices by limiting supply. The analysis is made more credible and vivid by the author's first-hand experience in commodity trading and by his welcome subjective and accessible style of writing.

Professor Raphael Kaplinsky, Fellow at the
Institute of Development Studies (IDS), University of Sussex

Globalization manifests itself in the poverty of Third World producers that enriches those who feed upon them. Peter Robbins provides a compelling account of tropical commodities, arguing for policies that might make for significant differences.

Ben Fine, Professor of Economics,
School of Oriental and African Studies (SOAS), University of London

Peter Robbins effectively demolishes the myth that international markets serve poor countries well, and proposes an exciting and workable new solution to the crisis facing primary commodity producers.

Dr Claire Melamed, Senior Policy Officer, Christian Aid

This is a welcome addition to the literature on the crisis in developing country agriculture. The book takes a radical position in support of active multilateral intervention – in the form of commodity pricing agreements – to secure decent livelihoods for the people who do the growing. This proposal, put forward by a former commodity trader – a poacher turned gamekeeper – deserves to be listened to and argued with.

Robert Jenkins, Professor of Political Science,
Birkbeck College, University of London

About this Book

Fifty or more developing countries still depend mainly on the tropical commodities or minerals that they produce. Over the past half century, it has become abundantly clear that:

- Encouraging so many countries to grow coffee, sugar, cotton and other crops has been a disaster.
- Small farmers get only a tiny share of the final tag on these commodities on supermarket shelves in the North.
- Prices have collapsed; terms of trade between North and South have deteriorated.
- And in their wake, living standards, foreign exchange earnings, tax revenues, and economic growth in developing countries have plummeted.

This up-to-date investigation by one of the leading authorities on commodity trading examines the way in which this situation has come about, the continuing importance of primary commodities to so many developing countries, and current trading arrangements.

The author looks into the possible solutions being proffered – from ideas to exploit new niche markets and improve quality, to more radical notions like fair trade – and shows how they all fail to measure up to the scale of the disaster facing the Third World. Instead, he argues, developing countries must take a leaf out of supply-side economics, and themselves take the measures required to bring supply and demand into a better balance that will secure for them far higher and more stable prices than today's.

Here is a crisp analysis of one of the most important questions in international economics, together with concrete proposals to establish a new supply management programme that, if acted upon by the countries of the South, could revolutionize their development prospects.

About the Author

Peter Robbins was a commodities trader in the City of London for thirty years. He was able to retire from that business early and became a consultant to the United Nations on trade relations between African countries and multinational companies. He then worked as an adviser to the African National Congress on trade sanctions against apartheid in South Africa. He is now working on establishing market information systems for tropical agricultural products in rural areas of Africa.

He has published several books on metals and agricultural markets and apartheid, which include *Trading in Metals* (Metal Bulletin, 1984); *Tropical Commodities and Their Markets* (Kogan Page, 1995); *Review of Market Information Systems in Botswana, Ethiopia, Ghana and Zimbabwe* (Technical Centre for Agriculture, 2000). He has also contributed to *After Apartheid – Renewal of the South African Economy* (University of York and James Currey, 1998); *The Sanctions Report* (The Commonwealth Secretariat, Penguin Books, 1990); *Sanctioning Apartheid* (Africa World Press, 1999); *A Framework for Macroeconomic Policy in South Africa: Making Democracy Work* (Centre for Development Studies, South Africa, 1993).

STOLEN FRUIT

The Tropical Commodities Disaster

PETER ROBBINS

ZED BOOKS
London & New York

UNIVERSITY PRESS LTD
Dhaka

WHITE LOTUS CO. LTD
Bangkok

FERNWOOD PUBLISHING LTD
Nova Scotia

DAVID PHILIP
Cape Town

BOOKS FOR CHANGE
Bangalore

Stolen Fruit was first published in 2003 by

In Bangladesh: The University Press Ltd, Red Crescent Building,
114, Motijheel C/A, PO Box 2611, Dhaka 1000

In Burma, Cambodia, Laos, Thailand and Vietnam:
White Lotus Co. Ltd, GPO Box 1411, Bangkok 10501 Thailand

In Canada: Fernwood, 8422 St Margaret's Bay Rd (Hwy 3),
Site 2A, Box 5, Black Point, Nova Scotia, Canada B0J 1B0

In India: Books for Change, 139 Richmond Road, Bangalore 560 025

In Southern Africa: David Philip Publishers (Pty Ltd),
99 Garfield Rd, Claremont 7700, South Africa

In the rest of the world:
Zed Books Ltd, 7 Cynthia Street, London N1 9JF UK and
Room 400, 175 Fifth Avenue, New York, NY 10010, USA

Distributed in the USA exclusively by Palgrave Macmillan, a division of
St Martin's Press, LLC, 175 Fifth Avenue, New York, NY 10010

www.zedbooks.co.uk

in association with the ACP–EU Technical Centre for Agricultural and Rural
Cooperation (CTA), Postbus 380, 6700 AJ Wageningen, The Netherlands

Copyright © Peter Robbins, 2003

The right of Peter Robbins to be identified as the author
of this work has been asserted by him in accordance with the
Copyright, Designs and Patents Act, 1988

Second impression, 2004

Cover designed by Andrew Corbett
Designed and typeset in Monotype Bembo by Illuminati, Grosmont
Printed and bound in the United Kingdom by Cox & Wyman, Reading

A catalogue record for this book is available from the British Library
US CIP data is available from the Library of Congress
Canadian CIP data is available from the National Library of Canada

ISBN 1 55266 111 3 Pb. (Canada)
ISBN 81 87380 82 9 Pb. (India)
ISBN 0 86486 634 8 Pb. (Southern Africa)
ISBN 1 84277 280 5 Hb. (Zed Books)
ISBN 1 84277 281 3 Pb. (Zed Books)

Contents

Introduction

Tropical agriculture is wonderfully diverse. The beautiful blossom of the night-flowering cananga tree must be gathered at dawn to be distilled into the ylang-ylang oil much prized by the world's perfume makers. Seven thousand tonnes of annatto seed is grown every year for the colouring of cheese. The people of Ethiopia make their bread from teff, a tiny seed first domesticated 10,000 years ago. Indian farmers harvest shellac, the main ingredient of French polish, which is excreted by minute insects. Some plants are grown for food, some for medicine and others for poison.

Agriculture is still, by far, the worlds' largest industry. Most of the 1.5 billion people who make their living from farming live in developing countries in the tropical regions of the world and work tiny plots of land using hand tools. These farmers must still cope with all the problems that farmers have faced throughout history – drought, storms and floods. Their crops are ravaged by insects, parasites, rodents and birds. If they produce too little, they starve. If too much is produced the market price for their crop falls and they are lucky if they can sell any surplus. They sweat from dawn till dusk in backbreaking work merely to survive.

Remote as this world may seem through Western eyes, tropical farming is inextricably linked to the global economy. But globalisation is not a new concept for Third World farmers. The cultivation of bananas spread from Southeast Asia to Africa in prehistoric times. Captain Bligh collected breadfruit from Tahiti and introduced it to the Caribbean in 1792. Crops like rubber, cocoa, maize, tomatoes, pineapple, cashew nuts, sunflower, vanilla, groundnuts and tobacco originated in the Americas but are now grown throughout the tropics. Brazil produces more coffee than any other country, but the coffee plant came originally from Ethiopia. Some of Europe's greatest cities were founded on wealth derived from trade in tropical oils, fibres and spices.

Since World War II, countries in the industrialised world have enjoyed an unprecedented period of economic growth. World demand continues to grow for more and different and better products. Supplies of raw materials and ingredients from tropical regions flow into the industrialised world at an ever-increasing rate. The rich world wants natural ingredients for polishes, pesticides, medicines, cosmetics, building materials, perfumes, food colourings, flavourings and thickeners. They want strawberries in December and apples in April. They eat more chocolate and drink more coffee. As their taste in food widens they import more spices, exotic fruits and nuts.

We could be forgiven for thinking that this burgeoning demand for tropical commodities would have benefited the millions of farmers who produce them – but it hasn't. Just as it seemed that tropical countries might have been given the opportunity to take a share of the growth in the world's economy, prices for their main export commodities have slumped to their lowest levels for decades. The value of a tonne of sugar, cotton or rubber is only about one-fifth of what it was twenty years ago. The value of coffee, on which 25 million people depend for a living, has fallen to one-seventh of its value in 1980. Most of the world's other major tropical commodities are worth less than half of what they were worth twenty years ago. The idea of cutting wages for workers in an industrialised country to a fraction of what they were in 1980 is unthinkable, but this is exactly what has happened to tens of millions of farmers in the developing world.

Tropical countries were plundered for their natural resources by their European colonial masters for several centuries. Their nominal independence left them with largely uneducated populations and very few modern industries. A combination of poverty and irresponsible leadership has led to conflicts in which tens of millions of people have died and many more have been displaced from their homes. Weather conditions in the tropics are becoming increasingly erratic due to global warming and more frequent El Niño conditions. Many of these countries are being decimated by HIV/AIDS and other diseases. Most farmers have no other means of making a living. In these circumstances we should not be surprised by the levels of poverty in the countryside of the developing world. Most farmers count themselves lucky if they can earn a dollar a day.

And now a new disaster threatens these fragile economies which are already burdened with massive debt. If the prices of tropical commodities remain at their current low levels, millions of the world's poorest people will be denied the basic human right to work for a living income. They will be locked into poverty and aid-dependency. They will continue to have no access to basic medical services, their children will not be educated, and they will lose all hope for the future. Any opportunity for many developing countries to participate successfully in the commercial life of the planet will be closed. It is a disaster of enormous proportions. Martin Khor Kok Peng of the Third World Network, a leading expert on development, has described the crisis as not only the world's most important trade issue but also the most important development problem.

The collapse of tropical commodity prices represents the most formidable obstacle to efforts to lift huge numbers of people out of poverty and yet, mysteriously, the problem has received almost no attention from the world's mainstream media. The reason for this may become clearer as this account of the problem unfolds. This apparent lack of interest should concern us deeply but we should be far more concerned that the governments of wealthy countries and the powerful development agencies that are charged with the task of relieving poverty appear to have no intention of recognising – much less doing anything to address – the problem, which is well within their capacity to solve.

The fall in the international prices of tropical commodities over the last two decades is inextricably linked to a change in domestic and international economic thinking. Prior to this period there was a broad consensus that some intervention by governments and international trade regulators was necessary to curb negative effects of market forces in order to protect the weaker and more vulnerable sectors of society. International agreements were established to prevent the prices of the major tropical commodities falling below certain agreed levels. In addition, the governments of developing countries were expected to prioritise investment in social capital – education, training, health and food security. They were also expected to provide some protection of their embryonic industries and were not required to compete, tooth and nail, with much more powerful nations in the jungle of international trade. In the last twenty years this consensus has been reversed.

The economic doctrine behind this change is not new but has reappeared in several guises – neoliberalism, School of Chicago, Friedmanism, Thatcherism, monetarism, non-interventionist, supply-side economics. Call it what you will, the fundamental idea is that economic growth can only be assured through unfettered, competitive trade driven by the requirement or whim of consumption. This concept must be adopted by all countries, rich and poor. The doctrine has become so widespread and deeply embedded that it now dominates all of the many other schools of economic thought. This economic approach is advocated by all the major financial and commercial institutions for reasons of self-interest but it has been lent much respectability by the Nobel prizewinning economists who have refined it and applied it to government and international trade policy. There is no doubt that the defenders of these theories will go a long way to avoid admitting any major flaw in their thinking.

We may be concerned that industrial countries are not doing enough to relieve the suffering of our fellow human beings in the Third World, but could it really be true that the governments of the rich world are coldly and deliberately causing the prices of tropical commodities to fall? No one could deny that the fall in the cost of importing these goods has benefited industrial countries to the tune of billions of dollars. You may conclude, after reading this book, that this saving is a factor which goes some way to explain why almost nothing is being done to bring this crisis to an end.

What is clear is that, if an analysis of the tropical commodities crisis leads to the conclusion that orthodox economic thinking is worsening rather than improving the economies of some of the least developed countries of the world, it will severely challenge the credibility of that doctrine. Those who impose economic policies on countries whose populations teeter on the edge of abject poverty bear an enormous responsibility and we must all be absolutely certain that these policies offer the best solution to the needs of the poorest section of the world's population. The lack of response to the tropical commodities crisis is an example of profound indifference on behalf of the industrialised world to the predicament of the world's poor. More importantly, I believe, it undermines the credibility of the dominant economic ideology of our times.

To understand how this crisis is linked to the evolving relationship between developing countries and the powerful forces that dominate international trade, it is necessary to examine the history of these relationships and to analyse the obstacles that must be overcome if a solution to the problem is to be found.

This book attempts to trace the origins of the crisis, to describe its effect and to outline what I believe to be the only rational way of dealing with it.

I have for a number of years now tried to bring this issue to a wider audience and to provoke some response from governments and development agencies. In the last few months of 2002 news of the crisis and its hideous dimensions began, at last, to filter into the more progressive areas of the mass media. In addition, some individuals in powerful organisations seemed to be on the point of making a breakthrough in stimulating negotiations to find solutions to this problem. In the final chapter I offer an account of my experiences as an illustration of how difficult it has been to bring about a real examination of this tragedy.

This story need not end in disaster, however. Developing countries have a group of resources – in the form of agricultural products which can only be produced in tropical regions – that the developed world cannot, or will not, do without. There is no reason why this card should not be played much more effectively in the game of international commerce. By exercising proper control of the production and export of the supplies of these commodities, tropical countries could earn hundreds of billions of dollars of extra revenue – far more than they receive in aid funding. These countries could introduce this radical new strategy to tackle rural poverty, to break away from aid dependency and to build a sustainable economic future.

In finding a way to maximise the value of this natural endowment all developing countries, from the Americas around the globe to Africa and the Pacific, will have to work closely with each other to manage the markets of their most important agricultural products. This will not be a simple task but, if they can reach agreement, they could reverse the present crisis and make a massive contribution to the welfare of their people.

CHAPTER I

WINNERS AND LOSERS

The scale of the decline in tropical commodity prices

The price, in dollar terms, for a tonne of most tropical commodities[1] is lower now than it was twenty years ago – much lower, in the case of coffee, cocoa, rubber and sugar, four of the most important commodities grown in the tropics (see Table 1.1). But even this comparison fails to illustrate the full scale of the decline in tropical commodity prices, because the value of each dollar earned in 2002 from the sale of these products was significantly eroded over this twenty-year period.

Agricultural commodities are sold to earn money to buy things. Farmers need tools, fertilisers and pesticides. They also need to buy clothes and medicines and they must pay for the use of vehicles to transport their goods to market. The cost of these manufactured products, many of which have to be bought in US dollars from industrialised countries, has risen considerably over the last two decades due to inflation. In order to appreciate the full scale of the loss of farm income, therefore, it is necessary to compare the buying power of the income derived from the sale of their crops in 1980 with that of 2002.

On average, any item purchased for $1 in 1980 would have cost $2.18 in 2002. Of course, farmers do not spend all their income on imported manufactured goods and some items, like

Table 1.1 Commodity price changes since 1980 (US$/tonne)

	1980	2002
Copra	415	260
Coconut oil	660	420
Palm oil	617	312
Sugar	254	126
Cocoa	2,832	1,190
Coffee	3,989	1,234
Tea	1,863	1,920
Pepper	1,974	1,550
Groundnuts	945	650
Jute	369	400
Cotton	1,675	793
Rubber	1,430	650

Source: Public Ledger, 24 April 1980 (£1 = US$2.257) and 22 April 2002 (£1 = US$1.4474).

radios, have not increased in price at average inflation rates. Most of these farmers grow their own food and the inflation rate of the costs of local services, like education, may not have been as high as dollar inflation. Using this measure, however, we can get a better idea of just how far the spending power of tropical farmers, who were already very poor in 1980, has drifted behind the spending power of the citizens of industrial countries (see Table 1.2).

The fall in value of tropical commodities has not been spread evenly over the last two decades. Prices have fluctuated up and down but the general trend has been downwards. Price decline has accelerated in more recent years. The World Bank's monthly index for prices of beverage commodities (coffee, cocoa and tea) shows a decline of 71 per cent between 1997 and 2001. The Food and Agriculture Organisation's (FAO) Food Index shows a 38 per

Table 1.2 Commodity price changes since 1980, taking inflation into account (US$/tonne)

	1980 prices adjusted for inflation	2002 prices	2002 as % of adjusted 1980
Copra	904	260	28.8
Coconut oil	1,439	420	29.2
Palm oil	1,345	312	23.8
Sugar	553	126	22.8
Cocoa	6,174	1,190	19.2
Coffee	8,696	1,234	14.2
Tea	4,061	1,920	47.3
Pepper	4,303	1,550	36.0
Groundnuts	2,060	650	37.5
Jute	804	400	49.7
Cotton	3,656	793	21.1
Rubber	3,117	650	20.9

Note: Goods bought for $1 in 1980 would cost $2.18 in 2002.
Source: Federal Reserve Bank of Minneapolis.

cent decrease in prices of food crops between May 1996 and April 2002.

Estimating the loss

It is reasonable to assume that, had producing countries been able to restrict exports of tropical agricultural products, the price of each commodity would be considerably higher than they are today. We know that the price of all commodities rises if supplies are restricted. For example, a severe frost seriously damaged an entire coffee harvest in Brazil, which had an impact on the world coffee market for a brief period between the end of 1994 and the early part of 1995. The fall in Brazilian supplies caused a sharp increase in the price of coffee to over US$2 per pound – four times the 2002 price.

Tropical countries export at least two hundred different commodities, all of which have been affected, to a greater or lesser degree, by overproduction. Some of the markets of these commodities are very large – 55 million tonnes of bananas are produced every year – while others, like frankincense, with an annual production of about 300 tonnes a year, are very small. It would be quite impossible to estimate how each of these markets could have been controlled and what effect such control would have had on prices. We will never know exactly how much better off tropical commodity suppliers would have been if they had been allowed to exercise some control over the markets of the commodities they produce, but it might be possible to estimate the order of magnitude of this figure.

Let us make the assumption that supply control could have been exercised over just ten of the more important tropical commodities – copra, palm oil, sugar, coffee, cocoa, tea, groundnuts, jute, cotton and natural rubber. Let us further assume that the supply of these commodities could have been controlled in such a way as to cause their prices to rise in line with the average inflation rate of all other goods. Given that demand for these goods has continued to rise over the last many decades, this may be thought to be a reasonable assumption.

Using these assumptions and the price data in Table 1.2 we can see that, by taking the difference in price between that received by suppliers in 2002 and the price they received in 1980 adjusted for average inflation, and multiplying that difference by the annual volume of production for each of the ten commodities, we arrive at a figure for 2002 of US$242.5 billion. In other words, had the prices of these ten tropical products risen in line with inflation, suppliers of these goods would have received in 2002 alone almost five times the total world annual aid budget.

In Chapter 4, I explore ways to restore a proper balance in

Table 1.3 Annual loss to developing countries due to collapsing commodity prices (US$)

Commodity	1980 price adjusted ($/tonne)	2002 price ($/tonne)	Production (million tonnes)	Fall in price	Loss (billion $)
	A	B	C	A − B	A − B × C
Copra	904	260	4.774	644	3.074
Palm oil	1,354	312	17.046	1,042	17.761
Sugar cane‡	553	126	142.500	427	60.847
Cocoa	6,174	1,190	2.954	4,984	14.722
Coffee	8,696	1,234	5.954	7,462	44.257
Tea	4,061	1,920	2.622	2,141	5.613
Groundnuts‡	2,060	650	27.561	1,410	38.861
Jute	804	400	3.024	404	1.221
Cotton†	3,656	793	14.000	2,863	40.082
Rubber	3,117	650	6.668	2,467	16.450
Total					242.888

‡ Excl. USA.   † Excl. USA and EU.

Source: FAO, Public Ledger, Production.

these markets by controlling supplies of tropical products with the objective of raising prices. It would be unwise to suggest, however, that supply control measures could lift prices to any predetermined level, and the limitations of these measures are discussed more fully in Chapter 4. In order to understand how prices might be affected, it is necessary to examine how commodity markets work.

If the price of a particular commodity were to rise too much it might deter consumers from buying the product. To achieve optimum results the supply would need to be cut to a level that would stimulate a price rise and retain the volume of sales to achieve the maximum amount of income from selling the goods. This optimum result may not coincide with achieving the highest possible price for commodities.

It might be possible, for instance, to raise the price of coffee to US$20 per pound from the 2002 level of about 50 US cents a pound. In order to achieve this huge price rise it might be necessary to cut coffee production by 80 per cent. This may not benefit many coffee farmers, however, as they could only produce and sell a fraction of the volume of coffee they sell in 2002 and their overall income would fall. In addition, such high prices are likely to encourage more people to drink tea and other beverages. At US$20 a pound, it might also encourage chemists to find a way of producing artificial coffee. In other words, supply control measures should aim to strike a balance between achieving higher prices and retaining overall demand.

In addition to this consideration, it should be borne in mind that some of these products are consumed within the developing country that produces them. And some commodities might not lend themselves as well as others to supply control.

Speculation about what might or might not have happened if the more wealthy countries of the world had allowed and encouraged developing countries to control supplies of their agricultural exports will not help us to calculate accurately the benefits to producing countries which would arise from future supply control measures. The above calculation, however, must lead us to believe that the rewards of supply control could be very large indeed.

The importance of tropical commodities

The primary importance of agriculture for developing countries is, of course, food production. Even today a significant percentage of rural populations are subsistence farmers living outside the cash economy altogether. They eat what they grow and barter some of their produce for tools, cooking pots, lamp oil and other essentials. Most farmers, however, sell a part of their harvest for cash but must also rely on their own farming efforts to provide food for themselves and their families.

At a national level, the economies of developing countries depend on agriculture for employment. The agricultural sector, therefore, represents a component of economic activity (GDP). Agriculture also provides raw materials for local processing and manufacturing industries and for export revenue.

The economies of about eighty developing countries are dependent, to a greater or lesser extent, on agricultural products. African countries depend on agricultural commodities for 50 per cent of their export earnings and these commodities account for 80 per cent of the exports of highly indebted poor countries (HIPCs). These countries are the worst affected by falling commodity prices, which prevent them from meeting the debt sustainability targets set by the international community. As a result, they do not qualify for any debt relief on offer.[2]

The relative importance of different aspects of agriculture vary markedly between one developing country and another. Only 2 per cent of Nigeria's exports, for instance, are agricultural goods but farming employs 43 per cent of the population and agriculture accounts for 37 per cent of GDP. Only 7 per cent of the population of Réunion are engaged in agriculture but agricultural products represent 70 per cent of the country's exports.

Sub-Saharan African countries and some Pacific island economies are among those countries most dependent on agriculture for exports, but even some of those Asian countries with successful industrial sectors, like India and Indonesia, employ over half their populations on the land (544 million people, in India's case).

These figures show that some developing countries in the tropics have large agricultural sectors but consume, domestically, most of the output, mainly food products. They may earn their export revenue from manufactured items, mining, oil or tourism but agriculture employs a large percentage of the population. Such countries do not suffer in the same way as those dependent on the export of cash crops, but low agricultural prices are driving people from the land and causing these countries to be more vulnerable to food shortages.

Subsistence farmers are also affected by low agricultural prices because they are likely to have to barter more goods for the manufactured items they need. The flow of revenue away from the countryside also reduces the provision of local services such as transport and education. Although farmers feel the direct impact of falling prices, rural industries also suffer. Local shops and services go out of business because their customers, the farmers, have less money to spend.

The greatest impact of low price levels for agricultural products are felt by tens of millions of farmers growing cash crops for the export market, be they a palm-oil producer from a comparatively wealthy country like Malaysia or a cotton farmer in the Sudan.

The national economies of countries that are dependent on agricultural commodities for export revenue are especially badly damaged by falling commodity pries. Many of these countries are in Africa. Some 95 per cent of Burkina Faso's exports are agricultural commodities. The figure for Mali and Togo is 60 per cent, for Tanzania 63 per cent, for Chad 78 per cent, for Sudan 94 per cent and for Kenya 55 per cent, and there are many others with a very high export dependency on the industry. Some African countries are very dependent on just one exported commodity: 63 per cent of Malawi's export revenue comes from tobacco, 59 per cent of Chad's from cotton, 63 per cent of Ethiopia's and 84 per cent of Uganda's comes from coffee, and 45 per cent of Côte d'Ivoire's export income comes from cocoa.

Although overall dependency on agriculture tends to be lower in the tropical regions of South and Central America and Asia, several island states in the Caribbean and Pacific are particularly vulnerable to the fall in value of cash crop commodities. The Dominican Republic depends on coffee and sugar for almost half its foreign income, the Windward Islands are heavily dependent on bananas, and half of Samoa's export income comes from copra.

Farmers are not necessarily the very poorest sector of society in developing countries. Although few actually own the land they work, many have the means to feed themselves and often have the opportunity to sell surplus production. Farming does, however, represent by far the largest industry in the developing world and the industry represents the backbone of these countries' economies.

The life of small-scale farmers in developing countries is hard and repetitive. Their first priority is to produce food for their family. They are likely to plant a staple crop such as maize, sorghum or beans and, maybe, another food crop (or starvation crop as it's sometimes called), such as cassava, which will provide food even if rainfall happens to be inadequate that season. Most farmers try to produce a surplus to sell in the local market and, if they have the space, to grow a cash crop, such as coffee, tobacco or peppers, which can be sold to consumers in the cities or to exporters. Their lot is improved immeasurably if they can earn enough from their work to buy medicines, pay for their children to go to school and have enough over to improve their farm.

The massive erosion of tropical commodity prices over the last two decades has consigned millions of people to a life of increasing poverty. It has added greatly to unemployment and the flow of people from rural areas into already overcrowded cities. It has also encouraged the production of illegal narcotics and the breakdown of the cultural integrity of many nations.

Most of these countries are heavily burdened with debt, and their lack of export revenue means that their governments have had to adopt policies of extreme austerity and reduce expenditure on health, education and infrastructural development in order to service their debt commitments.

Beneficiaries of the crisis

Despite the very significant fall in the prices of tropical commodities, consumers in developed countries have not seen an equivalent fall in the cost of the items they buy which are made from these products; in fact, prices have risen substantially. A box of a brand of well-known British chocolates in 1980 cost £1.03 in 1980 and now costs £3.08. A kilo of sugar bought in 1980 cost £0.75 but retailed in 2002 at £1.24. The price of a 200 gram jar of instant coffee has risen by a similar amount from £2 to £3.99.

If the price of the raw material has collapsed and the price of the finished product has increased, where has the difference disappeared to?

A lot of the difference can be explained by the increase in the cost of transporting, processing and packaging the raw products. Much of the difference, however, has been reflected in the profits of the giant multinational trading companies that dominate the processing, distribution and trade in these commodities. Table 1.4 records the recent profits announced by some of the largest of these companies.

Table 1.4 Recent profit record of major traders and processors of tropical commodities

Date announced	Company	% profit increase	Account period
16/08/02	Cargil	131	2002 fiscal
15/02/02	Cadbury	12	2001
02/08/02	Unilever	33	1st ½ 2002
23/08/02	Nestlé	79	1st ½ 2002
26/04/02	ADM (oil crusher)	26	3rd ¼ fiscal
31/05/02	Suedzucker (German sugar)	17	2001/2 fiscal
14/06/02	Tate & Lyle	41	year to March
28/06/02	Tchibo (German coffee)	47	fiscal 2001
05/07/02	ConAgra (US ingredients)	22	fiscal 2002
19/07/02	Kraft	17	2nd ¼
02/08/02	Starbucks	20	3rd ¼ fiscal
11/10/02	Sara Lee (coffee)	21	1st ¼ fiscal

It should be borne in mind that the profits of many companies in other sectors of the economy were severely depressed in 2001/2 due to a worldwide recession. In such circumstances profits of these magnitudes are quite an achievement.

The cause of the price collapse

So why have the prices for these primary products fallen so sharply? The short answer is oversupply. Although demand for these goods has steadily increased, production has increased at a greater rate. As supply outstrips demand, prices fall. We need now to ask why agricultural commodities have been particularly susceptible to oversupply.

If factory owners in the industrialised world find that there are too many other factories producing the same item, causing the price of their product to fall below a profitable level, some factories shut down. The factory workers may need to be trained in other skills but they are quite likely to find another job with a new employer. Third World farmers do not have such opportunities. They have few skills outside farming and there is nowhere they can go to be retrained. Their surplus crops are their only source of cash income. They must continue to produce them no matter how low the market price for them falls. The markets for these primary products, therefore, do not behave in the same way as markets for most manufactured goods.

There have been many occasions in the past when the prices of various agricultural commodities have slumped. Sometimes this happens when growing conditions are just right to produce a bumper harvest. Sometimes demand falls in economic recessions when consumers cannot afford to buy the goods or when tastes change or cheaper substitutes appear on the market and consumers lose interest in a particular commodity. Equally, there have been times when shortages of supply or increased demand have caused prices to rocket. The supply of all crops fluctuates over the growing season. Generally, prices fall during the main harvest

periods as more of the commodity has to be absorbed by the
market. Weather conditions and disease also influence supply. Frosts
in Brazil affect the coffee market, hurricanes in Cuba can reduce
the supply of sugar, and 'witches broom' disease can devastate the
cocoa crop in West Africa. These events usually have a relatively
short-term impact on the market and are considered to be normal
market fluctuations.

The markets for tropical commodities continue to respond to
these factors and prices move up and down slightly on a daily
and seasonal basis. The reason why many people are so concerned
with the current situation is that these markets now appear to
have been locked into a state of permanent oversupply causing
prices to remain at rock-bottom levels for the foreseeable future.

Economists have an explanation for a general trend in the way
the prices of raw materials move in relation to the price of manufactured goods. It is known as the Singer–Prebisch Hypothesis.
The idea was put forward by Raul Prebisch and Hans Singer in
the 1950s that the costs of turning raw materials into manufactured or processed goods would rise at a greater rate over time
than the rate in the rise of costs incurred in the production of
raw materials. The control of the oil market by the Organisation
of Petroleum Exporting Countries (OPEC) has led economists to
revise the hypothesis to exclude oil.

In the 1970s and 1980s tropical commodity prices remained
comparatively stable. In order to explain the present crisis we
must ask what has happened over the last couple of decades which
makes market conditions so different from those in the past.

At one level it could be argued that the price of a particular
commodity is determined by changes in supply and demand. But
the markets for commodities don't exist in isolation from the rest
of the world. People might choose, or be obliged, to produce or
consume a different commodity. Governments might introduce
subsidies or taxes on the production or consumption of various
products. Investment might be available for the production of one
product rather than another for many different reasons. One

country might block the import of goods from another country with which it has a dispute. In other words, there are many wider factors that affect commodity prices, including national and international trade rules and regulations and economic policies. Over the last twenty years this wider economic environment has changed profoundly and it should be no surprise that these changes have had a major impact on the markets of tropical commodities.

In the 1980s a new doctrine came to dominate all other schools of thought in economics. Neoliberal economists spurned the idea of government intervention in commercial activities. They convinced politicians that economic growth could only be sustained by releasing the full force of competitive private enterprise, unfettered by government interference. Adoption of this concept involved a whole raft of policy changes (or reforms, as these economists preferred to call them). These included measures to 'open up' national economies to global competition by lowering trade barriers, such as import tariffs, and to allow currencies to become convertible against other currencies. The treatment also involved reducing supply-side costs in order to boost company profits and increase investment. This meant cutting direct taxes and taxes on profits and changing the law to reduce the restrictive practices and power of trade unions. The key to economic success, the doctrine maintained, was to encourage investment and to do everything possible to become competitive in a globalised market.

The value of having a mixed economy of both private and public sectors was also challenged. State enterprises were thought to be inefficient and bureaucratic. They represented monopoly control of certain activities which blocked the possibility of privately owned, more efficient companies taking over these sectors. The neoliberal recipe required governments to privatise government-owned companies, public utilities and even health and educational services.

These measures were designed to liberalise economies and to achieve growth by fostering global competition. The most powerful development agencies, the World Bank and International Monetary Fund, pressed developing countries to adopt these measures in policy packages known as structural adjustment programmes (SAPs). In a nutshell, the World Bank summed up the policies for SAPs as 'including less taxation of agriculture, putting exporters first, liberalising imports, privatisation and fiscal reform'.[3] Aid, loans and loan guarantees were made conditional on developing countries adopting these programmes, and without World Bank and IMF backing it became almost impossible for them to borrow money on the world's financial markets. At a multilateral level, this new orthodoxy manifested itself in efforts to reform the rules governing international trade and, ultimately, in the establishment in 1995 of the World Trade Organisation.

It should be borne in mind that, although they are nominally UN agencies, the IMF and World Bank are controlled by countries in proportion to their financial contribution to the organisations. This gives the USA, for instance, about a third of the voting rights at the World Bank.

As the people of developing countries have very little spending power, industries producing goods for domestic consumption were unlikely to attract investment. For this reason structural adjustment programmes put the need to boost foreign currency earnings at the heart of their objectives.

Clearly, these countries have no chance of competing in the international market in high-tech manufactured products or in providing sophisticated services to overseas customers. The designers of the structural adjustment programmes needed to identify those products where such countries had a competitive advantage. For some countries tourism showed promise, but in most cases the only products that could be produced for export at a competitive advantage were primary products, especially agricultural commodities.

This strategy might have worked if only one or two countries adopted it, but structural adjustment programmes called for all developing countries to adopt similar policies. The result has been an increase in world supply of tropical products which is too large for increased consumption to absorb. Prices have fallen, in some cases, to their lowest level in history.

Increasing exports of tropical cash crops has also reduced the ability of many developing countries to feed themselves. As more of the best available land has been used to produce these crops, less land is available for food production by small-scale farmers. Many of these farmers have had to try to work more marginal land, causing environmental damage and desertification.

While powerful industrial countries were imposing this formula for the development of agriculture on tropical countries, they made little progress to liberalise their own farming sectors. The new world order of trade rules bears the hallmark of all authoritarian systems. Those who make the rules do not necessarily feel that they have to obey them. Farmers in the European Union and USA receive approximately half of their income in the form of government subsidies. Industrialised countries now spend US$360 billion a year supporting their agricultural sectors. (In May 2002 the USA passed legislation to increase payments to US farmers by US$45 billion over the next seven years.) Surplus quantities of agricultural products in many rich countries are purchased at high prices from farmers and exported to the rest of the world at much lower international market prices. The difference in price is picked up by Western taxpayers. A significant proportion of this surplus production is disposed of by selling it to traders in the developing world. In order to achieve these sales, the goods must be offered at prices which are lower than those offered by local farmers for the same product. Farmers in poor countries simply can't compete with these massively subsidised imports.

Economists recognise that the markets for agricultural commodities produced in poor countries do not behave in the same way as markets for manufactured goods. Unregulated competition in these markets encourages a 'race to the bottom'. Farmers have nothing else to produce if they wish to earn some cash income and so they are obliged to produce more and more, no matter how low the price falls.

This problem has long been fully understood by governments and UN agencies, which began to address the issue as far back as the 1950s. Their efforts culminated in a set of international commodity agreements covering coffee, cocoa, rubber and sugar – four of the most important commodities produced in the tropics.

Within these agreements, prices were maintained between narrow margins which were acceptable to both producing and consuming countries. The agreements required the support of industrialised countries, as they alone were able to regulate imports and/or to provide the money needed to finance surplus stocks, or buffer stocks as they were sometimes called. In the 1980s, however, the USA and the UK made it clear that the very concept of these agreements clashed with their new, non-interventionist economic philosophy. They withdrew their support and the agreements were effectively terminated in 1989. The prices of the commodities covered by the agreements began their inexorable fall to today's low levels.

Faced with this systemic problem, agricultural development agencies have tried to help individual countries to improve their earnings from exports. They have suggested a number of solutions including niche marketing, risk management, quality improvement, fair trade, sales promotion, and so on, but these strategies have often only intensified competition between producers. Several major development agencies still support programmes to increase production of primary products using technical innovations to improve yields or implementing policy changes to offer incentives to farmers to grow a particular commodity. Side by side with the new doctrine of laissez-faire economics these agencies have been spending aid money to help some poor countries compete more aggressively with other poor countries. It could be argued that the distribution of this spending has a political dimension, as countries in danger of rejecting the market system or supporting other unacceptable ideologies have been particularly favoured.

It has now become obvious that tropical commodity prices will continue to fall unless the root cause of oversupply is tackled head on. Many developing countries are drifting further and further behind the rest of the world. Economic growth rates, where they can be achieved, are usually less than population growth rates. Many of these countries have a per-capita income of less than a dollar a day. The absolute number of people in poverty is increasing, causing political instability and conflict. The industrialised world is simply not prepared to make the massive transfer of resources to the developing world needed to begin to reverse this decline. The dominant motive of industrialised countries, in their push to liberalise developing economies, is to sell more of their own goods and services.

The way forward

Tropical commodity markets are particularly sensitive to oversupply. The current difference between oversupply and a balanced market may seem fairly modest, but it is large enough to have caused the price collapse. A cut of production of only a few per cent is likely to be all that is needed to drag prices back to the levels prevailing twenty years ago.

Every tropical country producing a particular product could, as they did before 1989, reduce production by this modest amount and, there is no doubt, prices would rise sharply. But such a strategy would, of course, fly in the face of current economic orthodoxy.

The following chapters offer a more detailed account of the relationship between agricultural commodity markets and economic development. The role of agricultural sectors in developing countries, from the point of view of the citizens of those countries, is clearly quite different from their role as seen by powerful industrialised countries. In what way could these differences explain the current difficulties in tropical agriculture? To appreciate the present crisis it is necessary to understand the history of tropical farming and its evolving relationship with the world's economy.

Notes

1. The price of the major minerals produced in the Third World have not fared any better than agricultural products. In 1980 copper was trading at US$2,120 per tonne compared with the 2002 price of US$1,600. Tin traded at US$16,000 per tonne compared with the 2002 price of US$4,285.
2. Pierre Berthelot, *Commodity Trade: The Path to Unsustainable Development*, Commonwealth Secretariat, London, 2002.
3. World Bank, *Adjustment in Africa*, Washington DC, 1994.

CHAPTER 2

A BRIEF HISTORY OF COMMODITIES IN DEVELOPING COUNTRIES

People have traded in agricultural goods for many thousands of years. Trade in spices, oils, natural medicines, drugs, fragrant gums, wine, silk and tea has moulded our history and shaped our political landscape. Dhows and galleons, packhorses and camel trains established ancient trade routes for these products from China to India, from Nubia to Rome and from Peru to Cadiz. The history of trade is also a story of conquest and subjugation.

The most recent period of European colonisation began in the fifteenth century. Portugal, Spain, France, Belgium, Britain and Holland, followed by Germany and Italy, carved up the world's tropical lands between them. They subdued indigenous populations and plundered the land for its natural resources. They soon recognised the potential of agriculture in these regions and began to establish farms and plantations. The slave trade provided the labour they needed to meet their burgeoning demand for cotton, jute, tobacco and sugar.

In the late nineteenth century the Europeans drove the first railways deep into the interiors of the continents they had colonised and began to delineate national borders accurately. The railways and roads they built were designed to carry products from the interior to the coast, not to encourage or facilitate trade within the region. Borders between countries are now largely arbitrary, from the indigenous population's point of view, and they often cut across the territory of populations with a common language and culture.

European companies dominated import and export trade in tropical products, often holding a monopoly in specific commodities. Many of these companies not only organised the production of these goods but also transported them and processed them locally or, more often, in their home country. Some, like the giant chocolate, tea, sugar, tobacco and coffee companies, also marketed the finished product. In order to protect these monopolies trade barriers had to be erected between countries colonised by different European powers. Throughout the colonial period the Europeans fought each other for control over land and trade routes.

As urban populations in these countries grew and the number of plantation workers increased, the Europeans found it necessary to organise the distribution of food through governmental structures and to control wholesale and retail trade.

Independence

Wars of independence established self-governing republics in many Latin American countries in the nineteenth century. The process of decolonisation in Africa and Asia began after World War II and most countries had gained their independence by the end of the 1960s.

The ex-colonies generally retained the marketing structures and trade barriers bequeathed to them by the colonial regime, but they benefited from the relatively high commodity prices at the time. In the 1970s and early 1980s some commodities, such as coffee, cocoa, sugar and rubber, were the subject of International Commodity Agreements which maintained prices at a level agreed by producing and consuming countries.

Meanwhile, in the post-World War II period, European countries embarked on programmes to develop their own agricultural sectors, partly in response to their experiences in the war, when large quantities of food had to be imported by sea at great cost both in money and lives. All developed countries were able to boost agricultural output through innovations in farming technology – machinery, artificial fertilisers, pesticides and new multiplication techniques – financed by huge government subsidies. Farms in the industrialised world became bigger and more efficiently managed. During this period, developed countries also enjoyed unprecedented rates of industrial and economic growth. Trade in manufactured goods and services increased enormously. Transport systems improved by air, sea and land and communications technologies were developed to facilitate trade. Trade in raw materials and agricultural products had, by the late twentieth century, become a relatively minor component of international commerce. Farming now represents only about 2 or 3 per cent of total economic output in the most highly developed countries.

Modern farming methods have been slowly introduced into some developing countries. After gaining independence from their colonial masters, some countries were able to adopt modern farming techniques to boost output and increase the quality of their agricultural products. Large farms, plantations and ranches owned by white farmers in Southern Africa and Kenya were as efficient as those in the developed world. The large plantations of some Southern Asian and Latin American countries provided the revenue for investment to establish large and flourishing industrial and service sectors. Large-scale farming in these countries was often achieved at great cost to the local population, who were thrown off their land and either re-employed as farm labourers or forced into cities or onto marginal land thought unfit for commercial farming.

The vast majority of farmers in developing countries, however, lack the knowledge and investment to utilise modern farming technology. The traditional farming methods used by typical small-scale farmers in developing countries do not lend themselves so easily to efficient large-scale production. Uganda has roughly the same population as Holland and eight times its land area. Some

85 per cent of Ugandans work on the land but only 4 per cent of Dutch people work on farms. Dutch agricultural output, however, is five times larger than that of Uganda – US$14 billion against US$2.7 billion.[1]

In most tropical countries the modern farming sector is very small. There are two interrelated reasons for the slow uptake of modern farming techniques (of course, the degree of commercialisation varies from country to country). First, there are cultural reasons. Tribal traditions, especially in Africa, often give the control of land use to tribal chiefs and elders. The chiefs, in turn, are obliged to maintain the coherence of the tribe or clan and must distribute the use of the land under their control to each family in accordance with their need and status. This makes it difficult for them to hand over large tracts of land to a single commercial farmer or agricultural company. Establishing farming co-operatives also often conflicts with tribal tradition.

Second, there are economic reasons. The conversion from small-scale to large-scale farming in Britain in the eighteenth and nineteenth centuries was not achieved without a great deal of pain, but the growth of their industrial sectors meant that displaced farmers and farm workers could find work in mills and factories. Investment in the industrial sectors in most developing countries has not been high enough to provide alternative work for the huge percentage of the population now engaged in farming. Wholesale conversion to large-scale, commercial farming would cause the disintegration of traditional family networks. These networks represent a social safety net and a system of wealth distribution in many Third World cultures. Such a change would, therefore, be likely to add considerably to the already growing numbers of people living in poverty.

Many different development strategies have been tried. Most Third World countries have endeavoured to encourage investment in other sectors – in mining, tourism and industry, for instance. In agriculture, producers have been encouraged to move away from basic subsistence farming and to generate cash income by growing more than they need for their own domestic use and selling the surplus to local traders to supply the national and international market.

Structural adjustment programmes

Agricultural development in most tropical countries has faced an uphill struggle for the last twenty years. In an effort to stimulate development many countries borrowed heavily from bodies such as the IMF and from the commercial banking sector. Loans were not granted without strings attached, however. These countries were obliged to liberalise their economies by adopting significant policy changes, often applied in structural adjustment programmes (SAPs). These programmes generally included a requirement:

- to devalue the currency (to discourage imports and make exports more competitive);
- to make the currency freely convertible with other currencies (to facilitate trade);
- to cut public expenditure (in order to lower taxes);
- to dismantle state-controlled marketing boards (to offer opportunities to the private sector);
- to privatise state-owned industries (to raise capital and stimulate competition);
- to cut import restrictions (to encourage local industries to become more efficient);
- to allow foreign companies to freely repatriate profits (to encourage inward investment);
- to boost exports.

The economists who designed SAPs were convinced that the only way countries could transform their economies was to encourage inward investment and earn foreign exchange to invest in infrastructure and lay the foundations for industrialisation.

These measures assumed that any country could compete in the world market if production and investment were concentrated in areas where they were deemed to have a competitive advantage. The only activity in which most of these nations could be said to have a competitive advantage in the world market was in the production of agricultural products and the exploitation of natural resources such as forestry, fishing and mining. The major flaw in this strategy was that similar advice was given to almost all tropical countries at the same time. Coffee-producing countries were encouraged to boost coffee production; sugar producers should produce more sugar, and so on. This resulted in overproduction of these commodities, which caused prices to plunge in the international markets. Economists call this phenomenon the *fallacy of composition* – less income is earned as more commodities are produced.

Another component of SAPs affecting agriculture, which many observers believe to have been counterproductive, was the requirement that governments should cut public expenditure. All too often this meant a cut in health programmes and education but also in agricultural extension services. These services were set up by governments to help farmers to protect their crops from pests and disease and to produce higher yields of better quality products. The funding cuts have tended to reduce rather than enhance the flexibility of the workforce and to curtail agricultural development. Overall, the record of inward investment in the agricultural sector has been poor and the ending of currency controls has increased opportunities for transfer pricing abuse (where companies over-price imports and underprice exports to reduce tax liability).

The most important SAP reform, affecting the distribution of agricultural products, has been the dismantling of state-controlled marketing boards and ending the practice of setting fixed purchase and sales prices for commodities. It was assumed that government control of markets had obscured the forces of competition in supply and demand in the economy. It was believed that a free-market system would unleash these forces and increase productivity. It would force producers to meet the demands of consumers both in price and in quality. Farmers would be able to buy inputs, such as seeds, tools and fertilisers, cheaper from competing suppliers, and the country as a whole would become more competitive in world markets.

Unfortunately, competitive and transparent markets did not emerge spontaneously.[2] Most Third World farmers have too little land to produce truck-loads of goods. Many farmers live in remote and comparatively thinly populated areas of the countryside. There is not enough business in many rural districts to encourage more than one trader to operate. Farmers have no means of communicating with the outside world or even the nearest town and are often unwilling to risk the investment of bringing their goods to market, resulting in considerable wastage. Laws may have been passed in most countries which ban collusion among traders to pay low prices to farmers and charge high prices to consumers, but there are often insufficient resources to enforce such laws. Most traders have little experience of free-market conditions and are reluctant to put their fellow traders out of business by seriously competing with them.

Government-controlled marketing boards also acted as intermediaries between farmers and large, international commodity-trading companies. Their trading experience and large turnover enabled them to extract reasonable terms and conditions from the traders. Now that marketing boards have been dismantled, individual farmers find they have little bargaining power faced with the might of a giant transnational corporation.

Some developing countries were not able to implement SAPs until relatively recently, but rates of poverty have increased even in the many countries that adopted these changes in the 1980s. Intense conflict, both within and between countries, drought, weather changes caused by global warming and the El Niño effect, and now HIV/AIDS have further weakened economic development. Most critics of the reform process, however, acknowledge that markets in developing countries must be made more competitive; although SAPs were designed to do that, they do not appear to have achieved that objective for those poor countries which are heavily dependent on agriculture. Advocates of SAPs point to examples of countries that have improved their economies after adopting SAPs but there are few in the Third World.

Globalisation

Tropical countries have exchanged goods and ideas with many other peoples of the world for millennia. In these exchanges cultural links have been established which have influenced life in the tropics at all levels – in religion, scholarship, the arts, technology, public-sector structures, the economy and agriculture.

The world as a whole has benefited in many ways from the free flow of ideas on so many aspects of human interest. Globalisation in these terms is nothing new and, provided that new ideas are accepted rather than imposed, most people have nothing to fear from an acceleration of the process.

Most of us, surely, would like to see a more harmonious world in which people try to bury their differences and cooperate in the fight against poverty, ignorance, disease, pollution and the environmental degradation of the planet.

In the last few decades, however, the word 'globalisation' has been more narrowly defined by dominant commercial interests as the inclusion of the world's entire population in a single, global marketplace. This prospect has been made possible by innovations in communication and transport systems and by the growing interdependence of nations due to economic sophistication and burgeoning output.

The establishment of a global market coincides exactly with the interests of the large corporations that dominate the world's service and manufacturing industries. They are aware that, once trade barriers are eliminated, their financial muscle will enable them to capture new markets for their goods and services in countries that once protected their less powerful local industries from outside competition. The global market is now in the process of being translated into binding international trade rules under the auspices of the World Trade Organisation. WTO members have agreed to reduce, in stages, the trade barriers between trading blocs of countries.

Expanding markets for giant corporations at the expense of small, local industries hardly amounts to a justification for the liberalisation of the international trading system, however. The liberalisation lobby continues to make much more ambitious claims for the doctrine. They are not content with claiming that trade liberalisation is a path to economic growth; they insist that it is the *only way* in which countries can expand and strengthen their economies.

Advocates of these changes have supported their ideas with volumes of evidence and theoretical modelling. At one stage they used the success of the 'Asian Tigers' (Taiwan, South Korea, Malaysia, etc.) as an example of the benefits of open-trade policies, until it was pointed out that these countries went through a phase of protectionism and government subsidy before being able vigorously to expand exports and trade.[3] The United States, itself, relied on protectionism to build its economy. Ulysses Grant, US president between 1868 and 1876, said that 'within 200 years, when America has gotten out of protection all that it can offer, it too will adopt free trade'.[4]

Supporters of this limited concept of globalisation have produced statistics to demonstrate that exposure to foreign competition achieves higher economic growth rates. Developing countries vary enormously, however. Indonesia has a population of 180 million while Tonga's population is only 100,000. Thailand has a burgeoning industrial sector while Burkina Faso has almost none and 92 per cent of its population lives off the land. Aggregating figures for such different countries doesn't tell us very much. In addition countries that liberalise their economies are entitled to greater access to credit and aid which, of course, has the effect of boosting the economy.

There is no doubt that the lowering of tariff barriers by consuming countries has offered more opportunities to exporters in developing countries. The exposure of local production to foreign competition has forced some producers in developing countries to become more efficient. The dismantling of government-controlled marketing boards has stimulated the evolution of the private sector trading networks which are an essential feature of a modern economy. These changes alone, however, do not address the immediate problems faced by most poor countries and are likely, in many cases, to be counterproductive.

A reform of the world's trading system which is designed merely to increase the volume of international trade need not necessarily represent a positive development unless we can be assured that the new trading system is equitable. For the governments of developing countries the important issue is whether this process leads to growth in their economies.

The success of these global reforms and internal liberalisation measures (for those countries that have adopted them) has been patchy. In a long-term analysis of economic trends in sub-Saharan Africa, Engberg-Pedersen et al.[5] found that adjustment situations had made little positive difference to growth or poverty alleviation. Using statistics collected by the FAO, the researchers found that growth rates in thirty-seven African countries were not significantly different in the years 1986–93, when economic structural adjustment policies had been applied, than they had been in the seven-year period prior to adjustment. Of the sampled countries, 24 per cent had better growth rates, 22 per cent had the same rate of growth and 52 per cent had worse rates.

It has now become clear that although a link between economic growth and the liberalisation of the economy has been established for some types of economy, it has not been established for others. Can growth be achieved in this way, for instance, by economies that are almost entirely dependent on agriculture?

In a World Bank-commissioned paper, O. Badiane and N. Mukherjee of the International Food Policy Research Institute made the following observation:

The growing (and seemingly established) consensus among development economists and policymakers is that outward-orientated developing countries grow more rapidly than those that are not. While the precise role of exports in improved total growth is not yet fully understood, mounting evidence suggests that there exists a strong positive association between export development and the acceleration of income growth. It should be noted, however, that the literature establishes a relationship between exports of manufactured goods and income growth, but is less assertive about the relationship between exports of agricultural goods.[6]

Most tropical countries have found it difficult to compete with more efficient foreign agricultural producers and many are suffering surges in the volume of imported raw and processed agricultural products which compete with domestic production. At the same time, any improvement in the level of these countries' exports of agricultural goods has not been sufficient to achieve significant growth in the economy as a whole. This may be due, in part, to the difficulties of complying with the high quality standards required by many importing countries. And, as we have seen, the prices of tropical agricultural exports have plummeted. Liberalisation has not improved food security either. The small cut in agricultural subsidies in the developed world has reduced surplus stocks of food, which has had the effect of reducing supplies available for food aid. This means that countries with a food deficiency must purchase supplies on the open market, thus weakening their economies still further.

Just as global liberalisation affects different countries in different ways, it has also produced winners and losers in different parts of the agricultural sectors within individual countries. Large, modern farms which are capable of producing and exporting a commodity to international quality standards have benefited from the fall in tariff barriers. Communities of small-scale, isolated farmers, however, which make up the majority of the population in many tropical countries, find it more difficult to obtain credit from commercial banks as they have no collateral. They also struggle to pay for farm inputs, such as fertiliser and seeds, which were often supplied by state-controlled marketing boards in the past as a prepayment for their products. Extension services have been significantly reduced and the value of their surplus production has fallen. They are especially vulnerable to changes in production systems. The establishment of larger farms and plantations in some countries in the name of efficiency has marginalised many rural groups, thus adding to the problem of unemployment, urbanisation and cultural disintegration.

The link between external trade and economic development is clearly very complicated. The influence of one on the other depends on many things, including the type of goods and services involved, the relevant strengths of the trading partners and the rules under which the trading takes place. These rules have been established and amended many times in recent history. Over the last decade this process has accelerated to include most countries in the world and a greater range of goods and services.

The reduction of poverty in the developing world is largely dependent on the reinvigoration of industry in those countries. Since agriculture is by far the largest industry in most tropical countries, economic development, at least in the short term, depends on finding ways to increase the value of agricultural output. The international prices of tropical products are therefore of crucial importance. If the prices of exported agricultural products increased, some of the extra revenue could be invested in the production of higher quality goods and in the processing of agricultural products to gain a higher value on the international market.

Many of the mechanisms which shape the environment of agricultural development – investment, credit, subsidies, tariff barriers, market mechanisms and domestic economic policy, now lie outside the control of developing countries. These mechanisms are established and regulated by the international community through bodies such as the IMF, World Bank and increasingly by the WTO. The process of liberalisation is highly complicated and by no means complete. The decisions made by these multilateral organisations reflect a mixture of theoretical objectives and the compromises of historical power relations. The future of agricultural development in tropical countries is inextricably linked to the decisions made in these forums.

Notes

1. World Bank website: worldbank.org.
2. Shepherd, *Market Information Services: Theory and Practice*, FAO, Rome 1997.
3. Amartya Sen, *Observer*, 16 June 2002.
4. Ha-Joon Chang, *Development Strategy in Historical Perspective*, Anthem Press, London 2002.
5. P. Engberg-Pedersen, P. Gibbon, P. Raikes and L. Udsholt, *Limits of Adjustment in Africa*, James Currey, Oxford 1996.
6. O. Badiane and N. Mukherjee, *Global Market Developments and African Exporters of Agricultural Commodities*, World Bank/International Food Policy Research Institute, Washington DC 1998, p. 2.

CHAPTER 3

FAILING STRATEGIES

Agricultural development agencies employ staff who are highly qualified in disciplines which were more relevant when the markets for tropical commodities were more equitable. They are trained to improve yields, design storage facilities, combat pests and breed varieties of plants that are more resistant to disease or more tolerant of adverse weather conditions. Although these experts often work tirelessly in difficult conditions to help improve the lives of farmers, they have very little understanding of how commodity markets work or how decisions made in forums such as the WTO affect the lives of ordinary farmers. Some agencies employ agricultural economists, but very few of them have any experience of buying and selling tropical products. They conclude that the failure of past efforts to maintain prices at levels which gave producers a fair reward for their labours means that no further efforts of this kind should be attempted. They do not enquire too closely as to why these attempts to bring some order to these markets failed but take the failure as proof that markets cannot be tamed. They are fully aware of the huge difficulties faced by farmers due to the fall in commodity prices but assume that the onward march of a globalised market is somehow beyond control by human agency.

For this reason, these development organisations have made

very little effort to question or challenge the changes in the global market environment that have caused the collapse of commodity prices. Instead, they employ most of their considerable talents in attempting to find a technical solution to the problem.

There are many hundreds of such agencies working in tropical countries. They range from the massive UN Food and Agriculture Organisation (FAO), based in Rome, which employs thousands of staff, down to tiny, local agricultural research stations employing only a handful of professionals. Some universities have tropical agriculture departments; many national and international charities and churches carry out agricultural development work; and most developed countries have their own overseas development departments working on agricultural problems. The World Bank, the IMF, the United Nations Conference on Trade and Development (UNCTAD), the International Trade Centre, the UN Development Programme, the World Food Programme and, of course, the WTO also have departments dealing with agricultural development issues.

There is almost no coordination between these agencies and, in the case of the very large agencies, very poor coordination between their various departments and branches. There are many instances of duplication of effort and of programmes designed by separate agencies which contradict each other. In addition, teams working in agricultural development tend to focus on the immediate problems of the group of farmers they have been assigned to assist. They may encourage these farmers to grow a new crop in one local area only to find that the additional supplies cause the national price of that commodity to collapse. They might encourage a government to institute policies designed massively to increase production of a particular crop, which has the effect of glutting the world market. Such was the case when the World Bank stimulated a huge increase in clove production in Indonesia in the 1980s and 1990s. The 'technical fixes' preferred by these agencies take several forms.

Technical fixes

Achieving higher yields

From the point of view of one particular group of farmers, improving the yield of the crop they grow could boost their income. Agricultural development agencies can help farmers to increase their crop yield in many ways. Some varieties of crops produce greater yields, and the agency might introduce these varieties or even carry out the necessary research to breed a new variety suitable for the specific soil and weather conditions of the area. Linking planting and harvest times to the correct weather conditions can improve yields and this may require the establishment of training programmes and better meteorological services. Weeding, fertilising, mulching and pruning often increase yields, as does pest control. Inappropriate storage can expose stocks of harvested crops to rodents, weevils and funguses, and a great deal of work is carried out to design better storage systems.

Although the vast amount of resources devoted to yield improvement might improve productivity and benefit individual groups of farmers for a limited period, the overall effect is, of course, to increase output, which adds to the global oversupply problem.

Cutting costs

For a high proportion of tropical farmers cutting costs is not an option. Most of their costs are measured in the sweat of their brow. They cannot afford pesticides, herbicides or chemical fertilisers, they don't employ anyone outside their immediate family, and they don't use power tools or motor vehicles. For those that do, however, costs can be cut in many aspects of their work. Farm chemicals are often used too freely. Lower levels of application often work just as well. Using animals for transport and traction can cut costs and provide dung for fertiliser. Concentration of production on one or two crops rather than several can increase economies of scale but may leave farmers in a vulnerable position if disease strikes the only crop they grow or if the price of that crop falls. All too often, however, cutting costs means cutting the wages, increasing the workload and lowering the standard of the working conditions of farm workers. There are many accounts from around the world of farm workers being exploited and of attempts to improve their position being ruthlessly crushed.

The effort to cut costs often only increases competition between farmers and does very little to improve demand for the goods they produce. This is because demand is affected by the retail prices of products, which usually bear very little relationship to the cost of the raw materials.

Diversification

In a twist to Marie Antoinette's infamous 'let them eat cake' remark, many agricultural development agencies, noticing the fall in price of a particular commodity, have advised farmers to grow something else. This has not been as easy as it sounds and has rarely succeeded in improving the income of the farmers concerned.

First, coffee farmers, say, know nothing about growing spices. They don't know where to grow them, which pest is likely to devour them, when to plant them or how much looking after they need. The agency, therefore, needs to spend a lot of money teaching farmers how to grow the new crop. They rarely make any investigations to find out where or for how much the new crop can be sold.

Second, the effect of introducing the new production on the market is to lower its price. More often than not, the limited budgets of these programmes means that they have to be directed at farmers producing a major commodity, say coffee, who are encouraged to produce a minor crop like a particular spice. The reduction in coffee production is insignificant as a proportion of total coffee supplies but the impact of the increased supply on a relatively tiny spice market can cause the price to drop significantly.

Increasing quality

The International Coffee Organisation, which represents most coffee-producing countries, has established a policy to encourage member countries to improve the quality of the coffee they produce. This programme includes making an effort to produce more of the higher-value arabica beans rather than robusta coffee varieties but also to improve the quality of beans produced. This mainly involves modifying post-harvest systems such as fermentation, drying and washing techniques and paying more attention to picking out unripe, overripe, deformed or diseased beans by hand. Handpicking defective beans is an incredibly labour-intensive and arduous task.

The idea behind this programme is that it is perceived that customers in wealthy countries have become more discerning in their choice of coffee and will pay more for a better quality product. Whether this is true or not, the overall effect is likely to be that higher grades of coffee become as oversupplied as ordinary coffee beans. Coffee farmers might find that they have made considerable extra efforts to raise the quality of their coffee only to find that its market value has fallen. This contradiction is likely to apply to quality improvement programmes in most other primary commodities.

Genetically modified organisms

Third World farmers lose a significant proportion of their harvest to various kinds of plant disease and pests. The growth of their crops is also inhibited by weeds. Some large biotechnology companies have developed genetically modified crops that can survive contact with certain pesticides and herbicides, which are usually produced by the same companies. The companies have concentrated on producing GM varieties of crops grown by large-scale commercial farmers in temperate climates such as maize, soya, rape and tomatoes. The companies are trying hard to extend the market of these products into developing countries. They have persuaded politicians in their own countries to join them in this effort. Some developing countries have come under considerable pressure, especially from US government officials, to allow the products to be introduced. Some of these officials have claimed that GM technology could solve the problem of food insecurity and could boost output, and exports, of Third World agriculture.

There is widespread concern that genetic components of GM crops could naturally cross over into the genome of other plants, including those weeds that the herbicides are supposed to eradicate. Although the scientific data are inconclusive on this possibility, it is certain that once genetically modified material escapes into the environment it cannot be retrieved.

Apart from the other objections to GM introduction, including cost and dependency on the companies that produce them, opponents of GM technology point out that there is no shortage of food, at least on a global scale. If there is a shortage, as the biotechnology companies claim, why is it that food crop prices continue to fall and why are thousands of farmers going out of business? Food insecurity is caused by a failure of distribution and the inability of Third World countries to buy food because they lack the necessary funds. Singapore produces almost no food but no one would suggest it has a food security problem.

In 2002 the USA used the food crisis in Central Southern Africa as an excuse to introduce GM maize as food aid to the region but the countries concerned were worried that farmers would plant the grain and insisted that the grain be milled before distribution. US officials feigned outrage that countries in such dire need could reject their largesse. This and other cynical misrepresentation by the biotechnology companies has served only to increase the suspicion that this aggressive marketing has little to do with feeding the world but is very much concerned with boosting the income of the biotechnology industry. Commenting on the fall in US grain exports, Dan McGuire of the American Corn Growers' Association said that GMO now stands for 'grain market outcasts'.

Market-linked schemes

Agricultural agencies have very little understanding of the practices of traders and do not trade goods in their own name. Some, however, have picked up on some of the more noticeable new trends in consumer attitudes. Many customers have a growing interest in where their food comes from and how it is produced. At the same time, they are reluctant to buy products without a guarantee of their safety and quality. These agencies have concluded that tropical products could be sold at higher prices if they conformed with these trends in consumer interest.

Organic products

As mentioned above, many Third World farmers cannot afford to use artificial pesticides and fertiliser. This means that their crops are organically grown. Given that there is a growing market for organic products, they should command a premium price on the market in industrialised countries. The customers for organic products, however, are unlikely to take the word of a Third World farmer or a development agency as a guarantee that the goods have indeed been produced free of artificial chemicals.

There are a few international agencies, such as the Soil Association, who have built a reputation for impartiality and whose certification is respected by consumers of organic products. These organisations need to inspect the land on which the crop is grown and monitor every aspect of production and packaging for a number of years before granting a certificate, and must continue regular inspections thereafter. The cost of this work is very high, especially in remote locations, and may run to thousands of dollars – quite beyond the means of ordinary farmers in developing countries. Nevertheless, some agencies have funded this type of certification procedure. The proportion of customers who are prepared to pay premium prices is growing but still remains limited to a few per cent.

Increasing production: letting the market rip

The reality of the situation, as it now stands, is that the tropical commodities crisis is seen by orthodox economists as a manifestation of how the market works. If the price of a commodity falls enough, the strongest, most efficient producers will survive and the weakest will go to the wall. As these weak producers go out of business, production will be cut and the market will, once more, balance with demand at a new market price. As we know, however, the markets for tropical commodities behave differently from those of most manufactured products. Small-scale producers have no option but to keep producing however low the price falls, as they have no other source of income.

Incredible as it may seem, many agricultural development agencies are still funding projects to boost output of tropical commodities. The tropical commodity crisis has affected coffee more than any other tropical product. Over the last decade, however, the French and German government-controlled development agencies have funded programmes to help Vietnam, once a minor coffee-producing country, to become the world's second largest exporter. The Common Fund for Commodities, a UN-linked organisation working with the International Coffee Organisation, is spending millions to increase coffee production in many countries.

The Panglossian belief of these organisations in the power of the market to produce the best of all possible results leads them to believe that those involved in production will be strengthened in some way by cut-throat competition. *The Economist* summed up the orthodox view very neatly in an article about coffee:

> instead of trying to prop up prices using intervention schemes, as Brazil and other coffee producers have been doing recently, low prices should be seen as an ally: eventually they will drive out inefficient producers elsewhere, and Brazil will be able to increase its earnings through greater volumes.[1]

That such policies would cause millions of poor people to lose their livelihood appears to be an irrelevance.

Fair trade

Fair trade has been elevated in some quarters as an answer to Third World commodity difficulties, but the very definition of the term is extremely vague. For this reason, perhaps, it is worth spending some time examining the idea.

Fair trade was first conceived in its present form by small, alternative trading companies linked to charities that, typically, bought and marketed handicrafts from developing countries. They realised that many customers, who were concerned about the conditions of farm workers in poor countries, would pay more for products like coffee and tea if they could be sure that the premium they paid was passed on to the producers and that, for instance, children and women were not exploited in the production process.

Some Dutch organisations have marketed coffee from developing countries for some years. Coffee from Nicaragua had also been marketed in the 1980s to support the besieged Nicaraguan economy and some British alternative trading companies had gained some experience of marketing the product. Coffee is a dry commodity and will keep for years if it's properly stored. Most coffee is produced by small-scale farmers and its price has been at low levels for many years. Coffee, then, became the flagship product for fair trade. There were many technical and marketing problems to be overcome before it was possible to offer the products to the public. In addition, there was no agreed criterion for choosing which suppliers to use.

Most of the raw coffee bean supplies to the fair-trade sector come from co-operatives of coffee farmers working in Latin America. These organisations are large enough and well organised enough to produce a high-quality product, complete the necessary paperwork and transport it to the docks. They also have democratic decision-making processes and existing structures that could be used to spend the extra income from fair trade on community projects.

The market for raw coffee beans in consuming countries is extremely limited, so the coffee, once imported, has to be roasted and vacuum-packed. More recently, soluble coffee has been produced by the fair-trade movement. In order to justify the initiative in terms of volumes sold, the coffee has to be made available through mainstream outlets such as the large supermarket chains. The coffee must be branded – that is to say, names for the products need to be agreed, labels designed, consumer surveys conducted and advertising campaigns launched.

In the end, the blending, processing, packaging, financing, insurance, labelling, advertising and retailing are all carried out in the consuming country. The cost of carrying out this work is extremely high, especially because the companies are dealing in comparatively small volumes of coffee. The coffee farmers receive approximately US$1.20 per pound for green arabica coffee beans (compared with the market price of about 50 US cents); the cost of the work done in the consuming country is as high as US$10 per pound for soluble coffee.

These costs are augmented somewhat by churches and other charities (and even government agencies), which have raised millions of dollars to produce and market the products. Ten years after it was first launched, fair-trade roast and ground coffee now represents about 12 per cent of the British market and about 2 per cent of the much larger soluble coffee market. Fair-trade coffee enjoys a similar share of the market in Holland but has failed to capture any significant market share in most other European countries. Earnings from the sale of the products represent the bulk of income for the alternative trading companies involved.

The idea has been taken further in at least one instance – chocolate made from cocoa beans supplied by a rather unwieldy Ghanaian co-operative. The suppliers have been given a share in the British fair-trade company which bought their cocoa and marketed the chocolate to retail outlets. They have no share in the private-sector companies processing, advertising, distributing or retailing the product.

Several more fair-trade products have been introduced more recently to the market, including tea and bananas. Some commercial companies have even launched their own fair-trade brands. Sales of the products are still minute compared with their mainstream equivalents, however. Oxfam, in its report *Primary Commodities – Trading into Decline* (2002), states that 'fair trade has not fundamentally changed world markets even in its core beverage sectors. Less than one per cent of total tea, coffee and cocoa sales are carried out on a fair trade basis.' The report continues: 'in Europe, at least, the rate of growth in fair trade goods is slowing down'. Fair-trade supporters were delighted when, in November 2002, the British Co-operative Society retail supermarket chain announced that its own-brand chocolate will be wholly produced from fair-trade cocoa beans. This new product will double UK fair-trade chocolate consumption to £6 million a year, yet the total UK chocolate market is worth £4 billion a year.

The income of tropical farmers would certainly be improved if everyone bought fair-trade products. The problem is that this isn't happening, and without a long and costly educational and advertising campaign, it is unlikely to happen. And there is a danger that the hype associated with fair trade will lead well-meaning people to conclude that they have done all that they can to address the tropical commodity crisis when they buy one of the fair-trade brands.

Appeal to multinationals and supermarkets

Some campaigners have made an assumption that the multinational trading companies and processing conglomerates could and would pay better prices for tropical commodities if they knew more about the difficulties caused by low prices. Naive as this assumption my sound, they have appealed to these companies to increase their purchase prices – so far without success. As can be seen from Table 1.4 some of these multinational companies have benefited enormously, partly from having access to cheap raw materials. They are very unlikely to assist in the killing of the golden goose.

Supermarket chains may be thought of as a 'softer touch' in that they deal directly with the public and so are more vulnerable to consumer boycotts and more likely to benefit from policies such as favouring poor producers if consumers appreciate them. They were won over to the idea of stocking fair-trade products with these arguments. It is often difficult to determine whether supermarkets are profiting from having access to cheaper products, however.

Most supermarket chains operate a system with their suppliers known as a marketing allowance or a retrospective discount. In this arrangement the supplier does not reduce the price to its customers of a particular item if they are making a high profit margin on it but instead remits an annual lump-sum payment to the supermarket. This allows the supermarket manager to use the money to cover the cost of loss leaders or losses made in error on other products. The scheme is much appreciated by supermarkets because it gives them greater flexibility in organising their business. It makes it almost impossible, however, for researchers to identify which products represent the largest profit-makers. It is commonly understood that the most generous market allowances are offered by coffee suppliers.

Niche marketing

Even very large manufacturers have recognised that some consumers will pay high prices for special or exclusive products. The wine and perfume markets demonstrate this phenomenon well. Japanese consumers will pay four or five times the normal price for some high-grown Jamaican coffee. The key to this marketing effort is in clever branding. The problem with this strategy, in so far as it could be used to improve the income of tropical farmers, is that supplies to a niche market, by definition, must be very limited. Much of the premium paid for these products is absorbed by branding costs.

Risk management

Another strategy adopted by development agencies, which belongs to a past era when markets were more equitable, is risk management. In those days, temporary price fluctuations caused difficulties for those who wished to sell their products on the world market. They might, for instance, agree to sell a commodity to a local agent in April when the market price was US$1,000 a tonne, only to find that the price had fallen to US$800 a tonne by the delivery date in June. These were often seasonal fluctuations as prices dipped during the main harvesting periods. Techniques were developed many decades ago which gave producers the ability to 'hedge' their transactions through the main commodities futures markets. This involves forward selling of paper contracts to back up the physical transactions and/or the buying and selling of 'options' – so-called derivatives.

These techniques could not be used to gain prices that were higher than the market price but could help to achieve sales in the higher price range traded over a market cycle of a limited period of time – typically three to six months. Each transaction involves the paying of a commission to a market broker and/or a premium for an option purchase and a returnable deposit to insure the broker against lack of performance. The broker would also have to be assured of the creditworthiness of the client. The minimum value for a transaction for coffee, for example, even at 2002 prices would be approximately US$18,000.

Clearly, no typical farmer in a developing country could afford to use these techniques. If they had US$18,000 they wouldn't want to continue farming. Some agencies, notably the World Bank and UNCTAD, nevertheless decided that they would try to make this facility available to small-scale farmers. They quickly discovered that commodity brokers were not prepared to take on any extra risk to help implement these programmes and so the agencies decided to take over the risk themselves. Only large farmers were able to produce enough to cover a minimum transaction on the futures market. This restricted the scheme to a tiny fraction of 1 per cent of tropical farmers. Nevertheless the offer to use futures markets in this way was extended to traders working in developing countries. The programme was strongly supported, at least in word rather than hard cash, by the brokers who stood to benefit handsomely from increased brokerage fees.

The only suppliers capable of using the scheme are large producers and co-operatives and medium-sized indigenous trading companies. Many of these organisations were already using futures markets in this way and so the scheme simply transferred the brokerage fees from them to the public purse. It has also helped a small number of groups and companies, whose resources were just less than those required, to use the markets in this way. It has helped, in other words, to turn some sub-Mr Bigs into Mr Bigs.

UNCTAD, having examined the benefits of their programme, have now all but abandoned it. The World Bank, disappointed at the level of uptake of the service, are contemplating paying the entire cost of options as well as covering any risks involved, much to the delight of the Wall Street brokers.

Sales promotion

Some analysts blame the appallingly low prices of tropical commodities on a lack of demand for the products. The Common Fund for Commodities, a rather strange relic of the International Commodities Agreements of the 1970s and 1980s, has a remit to assist developing countries with their commodity problems. Any effort to promote market intervention to achieve this objective, however, is outside this remit. They can, however, use their funds to assist producers with some of the strategies outlined above, including market promotion. The International Coffee Organisation is also funding its members' product.

Once again, there is no coordination of these initiatives. The Coffee Organisation, for instance, is not in the least bit concerned that extra coffee sales will result in lower sales of tea. The large multilateral processors of these raw materials are, of course, delighted to have their products promoted at the expense of the public purse.

Useful innovations

Although they receive little attention or support, there are certain strategies that are being followed that can increase the proportion of the value of tropical products received by the farmer.

Market information provision

Most state-controlled marketing boards in developing countries have now ceased to function. Prior to liberalisation, these boards monopolised the purchase of agricultural commodities from farmers at prices that were fixed by the boards. These prices were changed from time to time to reflect world prices but usually stayed the same for months at a time. In those days farmers knew what price they were likely to receive and could make decisions about which crops to grow accordingly.

Those who designed the economic liberalisation programmes assumed that free and transparent market systems would quickly evolve to take the place of marketing boards and that these new systems would return a greater proportion of the market price to producers. In most cases this has not happened. Traders encounter many risks dealing with small quantities of varying quality products, which they have to move over long distances on poor roads. To reduce these risks traders not only reserve high margins for themselves but also collude with each other to keep farm-gate prices down and retail prices high.

It was soon recognised that a free-market system could not work unless all the actors in the market were properly informed about market conditions and constantly changing market prices.

Most countries established agricultural market information services for this purpose. Unfortunately, almost all of them failed to provide the kind of information needed by small-scale farmers, traders and processors. The services tended to be overbureaucratic and expensive. They were used, almost exclusively, to provide economic data, such as inflation statistics, for government departments. Many have ceased to operate as donor agencies withdrew their support.

Most tropical farmers now have no idea of the latest price being offered for their goods in their nearest town, let alone in their capital city or on the international market. They have no access to telephones or other electronic communication systems. Many cannot read or understand the languages spoken in other parts of their country. They don't know who to trade with or what products are in demand. They are often not prepared to go to the effort and expense of bringing their products to market for fear of not finding a buyer, which leads to significant wastage. Their ignorance of market conditions allows them to fall prey to unscrupulous traders who agree with their fellow traders to pay only a fraction of the true price for the farmers' products.

Efforts are now being made by a few development agencies to establish market information services which broadcast up-to-date information on prices and market conditions through local FM radio stations in the language spoken by the people of an area. They work well only when local people are involved in the design of the service and when they help to identify the type of information they need. Very few donor agencies are prepared to fund these projects, however, having wasted millions on inefficient government-controlled services.

Collective action

Typical farmers in developing countries are limited in what they can produce. Only small areas of land can be successfully cultivated, by a single family, using hand tools such as mattocks and machetes. In any event, there is a shortage of suitable land in most developing countries. Most of the land they work is usually taken up with growing food for their own consumption. This means that any surpluses they may produce will be in tiny quantities – one sack of maize, one bunch of bananas, a few pounds of spices, at a time. They have few storage facilities and often have debts to pay, so they must sell these goods as soon as they are harvested.

No trader is prepared to send a truck to a remote farm to pick up such tiny quantities, and even when the farmers bring their product to market they cannot expect to get the price paid for a whole truckload of the same product. In order to obtain these higher prices it would be necessary for the farmers to improve their economies of scale, as the jargon puts it. This could be achieved by many farmers in a particular area getting together to decide which crop to grow; to grade and sort the product after harvesting to ensure a homogeneous product; and to market the larger quantity collectively – in other words, to work as a co-operative, just as viniculturists do so successfully in Europe.

The word 'co-operative' has negative connotations in many parts of the tropical world. In Ethiopia many farmers were dragooned into joining state farms, which became inefficient and corrupt. Elsewhere in Africa governments encouraged co-operatives and installed their own managers to run them. Many of these managers also became corrupt and often disappeared with the farmers' savings.

Despite this rather disappointing history many farmers have realised that collective activity can improve their lot immensely. They can pool what little cash they have to start credit unions. Commercial banks are often prepared to advance small loans to groups rather than to individuals. They can collectively afford to build stores in which to keep their harvested crops until prices improve. They can hire lorries to get their goods to bigger markets where prices are higher. More importantly, groups of farmers have much more bargaining power with traders than individual farmers.

Co-operatives have worked successfully in Latin American countries for many decades. The process of establishing farming co-operatives elsewhere in the tropics has been slow and difficult, partly because of past failures and partly because the farmers lack experience in managing any enterprise larger than their own farm. They may not trust any individual from the group to negotiate with dealers, collect proceeds and handle bank accounts. They need assistance from people who have the experience of working in successful co-operatives and can help them design the democratically controlled systems needed to agree on farming and marketing strategies, to record the contributions of the members of the group, and to administer the sale of goods, purchase of inputs and control of funds.

Some development agencies, too, are reluctant to help co-operatives get off the ground. One USAID representative in Uganda recently told me that co-operatives were 'socialistical'. They prefer to offer such assistance to groups with another strong common interest, the congregation of a particular church, for instance, or to groups with no pre-existing social cohesion, such as displaced people. Governments, too, are often reluctant to agree programmes to encourage the establishment of co-ops. They are suspicious of the political power that larger co-operatives might gain, which could compete with the structure of local government under the control of the ruling party.

Levelling the playing field

One orthodox response to the profound and acknowledged difficulties faced by tropical farmers has been to push for the removal of trade barriers for their goods. There is some merit in this suggestion. Let us take the example of sugar.

Of the 145 million tonnes of sugar produced each year, approximately 25 million tonnes are produced from sugar beet. Some 17 million tonnes of sugar are produced by European sugar beet farmers. Within the EU these farmers get paid almost twice the price for their sugar than they could get by selling it on the

world market. Only limited quantities of sugar are allowed into
the EU area and European sugar consumers must pay a higher
price for the product in order to subsidise their farmers' income.
Incidentally, the EU exports approximately 5 million tonnes at
the lower world price, thus undermining the price received by
farmers in the developing world still further. The EU's policy on
sugar is obviously 'trade distorting', but as yet there seems to be
no prospect of any immediate moves to end it.

If these trade barriers were to be eliminated, very few farmers
in Europe could afford to produce sugar. The market for cane
sugar grown in the tropics would, therefore, expand by 17 million
tonnes and the world price would, consequently, be likely to rise.
In the short term this might well be a better solution to the crisis
in sugar prices than the supply management approach, discussed
later in the book. There are markets of other products that could
be improved in favour of tropical farmers in this way – vegetable
oils, rice and cotton, for instance.

Then there is the problem of escalating tariffs. This term refers
to the practice in consuming countries of increasing the rate of
import tax levied on commodities in proportion to the amount
of processing they receive. The import tariff on raw coffee beans,
for instance, might be set at zero. The rate for roasted coffee
might be 5 per cent, for roast and ground 10 per cent, and for
soluble coffee packed in jars ready for retailing 20 per cent. The
benefits to the consuming country are obvious. They get the
cheapest possible raw materials but can sustain processing industries without fear of competition from the countries that produce
the raw material, as these countries cannot produce the processed
product cheap enough to overcome the tariff barrier.

Some consuming countries also impose higher duties on a
seasonal basis. They may want cheap fruit produced in tropical
countries in the wintertime but want to protect their own fruit
farmers when they harvest their products.

More insidious obstacles erected by consuming countries to
protect their agricultural and processing industries take the form

of non-tariff barriers. These can range from arbitrary assessments of quality leading to the return or destruction of imported goods, to an insistence on the presentation of complex certification, to the adoption of unnecessarily strict safety standards. Tropical producing countries have little say in how these safety standards are decided upon or enforced.

Such trade barriers are blatant examples of the hypocrisy of the developed countries that insist on the liberalisation of the economies of poor, developing countries. These barriers also serve to smother any opportunity a developing country might have to develop its own processing industries and condemn it to dependency on raw commodity production in perpetuity. Every effort should be made to reduce trade barriers which negatively affect the livelihood of farmers in developing countries, but even if this was done, it would not solve the price crisis for most tropical commodities.

It is not always fully understood that most exports of tropical products from developing countries are not affected by these barriers. For the raw form of these products, there is little or no import duty imposed by consuming countries. As has been explained, consumers in developed countries want to buy their raw materials as cheaply as possible and for imported goods there are no subsidies that have to be paid to local farmers.

Recently, several measures have been taken by developed countries that allow, at least in theory, full access to their markets for even the most highly processed goods from the forty-eight poorest nations – the so-called least developed countries (LDCs). The European Union has passed the 'Everything but Arms' initiative, which allows all goods, apart from sugar, bananas and rice, to come to the EU free of duty. The Africa Growth Opportunity Act, passed by the US Congress, offers a similar opportunity. Other measures taken by Canada, New Zealand, Norway and Japan offer similar access to their markets.

In addition, the WTO's Agreement on Agriculture required all countries, with the exception of LDCs, to lower all tariff barriers to trade in agricultural products and to reduce farm subsidies. The WTO ministerial meeting in Doha committed all members to lowering these protection measures still further. This process is by no means complete and we now find ourselves in an extremely unsatisfactory transitional stage where developed countries have lowered but not eliminated farming protection but retain substantial subsidies, while developing countries have also lowered their trade barriers but cannot afford farm subsidies.

To sum up, the elimination of trade restrictions imposed by consuming countries on the developing world would assist some farmers, producing some products in some countries to earn a better living. They should, therefore, be eliminated. The WTO has developed a theoretical timetable to achieve this end. If all members agree at each of several stages in the process, farm support and trade restriction might end in about eighteen years' time. Unlike the tropical commodities crisis, this issue is at least on the agenda. In eighteen years, of course, the tropical commodities crisis might have resulted, directly or indirectly, in the deaths of millions of people and the near destruction of many countries' economies.

Yet the problem isn't just the lethargy of the trade reform process, deliberate or otherwise. The problem is that the lowering of trade barriers and farm subsidies is not an instrument aimed exclusively at improving the market for tropical commodities. Another objective of this programme is to reduce taxes in developed countries. Another is to lower the income of workers in developed countries as they face increased competition from workers in the developed world. It is yet another manifestation of the narrow definition of globalisation used by neoliberal economists. The process threatens to lower still further the income of small-scale farmers in developed countries, which will reduce populations and amenities in the countryside of those countries.

The strategy is a blunt weapon. Reducing farm subsidies and tariff barriers on crops that are not exported in any quantity from tropical countries, like potatoes, wheat, barley, rye, oats, olive oil, wine grapes, and so on, will not put one penny in the pockets of Third World farmers. These measures might boost the income of large and efficient farmers in Australia, Canada, Chile and Argentina, but these are comparatively wealthy countries with mixed economies and a comparatively low dependency on agriculture.

In October 2002, British prime minister Tony Blair accused the French president, Jacques Chirac, of preserving the hugely expensive Common Agricultural Policy (CAP) at the expense of poor farmers in the Third World. The CAP, among other things, is the instrument used to deliver subsidies to European farmers. Chirac was reportedly infuriated by this accusation, but in the ensuing debate no mention was made of the tropical commodity crisis, which makes the residual problem of market access pale into insignificance.

If organisations like the WTO are to be used as the vehicle for introducing measures to bring some order to tropical commodities markets, it will have to adopt a framework which allows it to examine the problem associated with each commodity separately. Piling all the blame and cost of assisting Third World farmers on their fellow farmers in developed countries is neither useful nor equitable.

Other initiatives to help farmers

Some development initiatives other than those specifically directed at agriculture can, indirectly, improve life in rural areas. Programmes to improve roads and transport systems help farmers to get their produce to market but these programmes are progressing slowly, especially in remote rural areas.

Some agencies are providing and administrating micro-credit schemes for rural borrowers. Agriculture is, however, an intrinsically risky business, especially as prices are so low. The credit available tends to be taken up by small traders and micromanufacturers, who have some collateral and can make rudimentary business plans, rather than farmers. The sum of money available to each borrower is tiny, making the cost of administration and, consequently, interest rates very high.

One, more enlightened, analysis of rural economies has concluded that communities living in the countryside can reduce their dependency on agriculture by engaging in other kinds of activity. They could, for instance, start small engineering workshops to manufacture simple tools and repair vehicles. They could establish dressmaking and tailoring businesses or simple food processing workshops to supply the local community. These initiatives, of course, require training and investment, which is hard to come by on small development budgets.

Efforts to control corruption and to enforce laws preventing traders from smuggling goods and swindling farmers will also help to increase the income of rural communities.

Conclusion

The various programmes described above will go nowhere near compensating farmers for the loss of income they have suffered due to the collapse of commodity prices. At best a small number of farmers will be able to compete in the market more effectively with other farmers. Many of these projects only contribute to the problem by increasing supplies to an already glutted market. The fair-trade movement should be encouraged, not least because the organisations involved try to raise awareness of the plight of poor farmers around the world. It is better to buy a fair-trade product than a product produced by some giant multinational corporation. Customers should realise, however, that this incentive will not solve the commodities crisis.

Note

1. *The Economist*, 9 September 2000, p. 84.

CHAPTER 4

CONTROLLING SUPPLIES
AND TAMING MARKETS

In *The State of the World's Children*, J.P. Grant questions the assumption that rich counties alone should be given the right to manipulate market conditions. 'Action of this kind', he says, 'can surely not be rejected on the grounds that it interferes with the laws of the marketplace when the industrialised world itself continues to spend between US$125 and $150 billion a year[1] on agricultural subsidies which deprive the developing world's exports of the right to compete for markets and are essentially commodity agreements to stabilise and guarantee incomes of Europe's own farmers.'

It has now become self-evident that none of the various strategies currently being used to address the disaster caused by the collapse of tropical commodity prices will make a significant impact on the problem of oversupply. The obvious solution is to cut the volumes of supplies until they are, once more, balanced by volumes of demand at price levels that are high enough to deliver a fair reward to producers but not so high that they deter consumers from buying the products. In other words, it is necessary to manage supplies of these commodities.

This strategy would entail cutting the production of tropical commodities. Coffee, clove and cocoa trees would have to be cut down, pepper vines uprooted and a proportion of the fields once used to grow lemongrass, groundnuts, sugar, and so on, should be used to grow much-needed food. Simple as this may sound, the management of such a programme on a world scale would be a difficult task. Complicated as the logistical, administrative and political difficulties may be, I believe this to be the only solution to the tropical commodity crisis.

This is not a novel idea. Supply management systems were, and still are, commonplace. Until comparatively recently, marketing boards controlled prices and supplies of agricultural goods throughout Europe, in most developing countries, and in Japan and in the USA. Internal agricultural markets are still controlled by the Common Agricultural Policy and its US equivalent. The large multinational mining companies controlled the price of many different metals until the 1970s. And, as has been mentioned, even the markets of several important tropical commodities were managed in one way or another over many periods in the twentieth century until the end of the 1980s.

It is difficult to conceive of a commodity more difficult to control than gem diamonds. Millions of dollars' worth could be smuggled in a matchbox. Yet De Beers, the Swiss-based mining giant, has limited the supply of diamonds to meet demand at a profitable level for over a hundred years. Oil, the world's most important raw commodity, is successfully controlled by OPEC countries despite the huge political differences between them. Unofficially, producers of many products limit competition between themselves in 'gentlemen's agreements' by carving up the market between them or following each other in rotation on wholesale and retail price increases. Large trading firms regularly and substantially influence commodity markets through speculative activities. More generally, all countries implement a plethora of import restrictions, such as tariff barriers, to limit the supplies of foreign goods entering their markets.

Recently, aluminium and steel producers and the producers of certain basic chemicals have agreed to limit supplies in order to boost prices. Developed countries also face the problem of 'structural excess capacity' on a global level in these commodities. In the aluminium sector six producing countries agreed in 1994 on a memorandum of understanding to cut back on production in order to prevent prices from plunging further. In the steel sector the developed producing countries reached agreement in September 2002 to allow steel industries in their countries to cut production under the OECD umbrella. It is expected that this agreement will help the USA and other countries to resist pressure from their steel industries for the imposition of further anti-dumping duties on low-priced imports.

Market control systems are generally accepted as being a logical way of preserving jobs and ensuring a steady supply of goods. The role of international bodies such as the WTO and national bodies like monopolies commissions is to draw the line between accepting, on the one hand, market control, when it is perceived to be for the common good, and, on the other hand, rejecting profiteering arrangements when one or a few companies conspire to monopolise supplies. At times these may be difficult or even arbitrary decisions but, provided they are made by democratically controlled bodies, they are considered to be fair.

The argument used to propose or oppose supply management of tropical commodities, then, is not set in an arena in which rigid rules apply. WTO rules, for instance, may or may not provide a legal framework for global supply management of tropical commodities to take place but, ultimately, it is for the democratic process within the WTO to decide which rules to apply. The judgement is usually made, and should be made, by bodies which democratically represent those that stand to benefit from supply management and those that do not.

This leads us to question the degree of democracy operating in bodies like the WTO. We will return to this important issue later, but let us first discuss the likely nature of a programme that could be used to control oversupply and some of the difficulties that are likely to be encountered by those striving to establish such programmes.

A model for establishing and administrating supply management programmes for tropical commodities is lying on the shelf.

It only needs to be taken down and dusted and it could be ready for use. The UNCTAD-inspired international commodity agreements ended just over a decade ago and many of the people who administrated the agreements are still around and could be encouraged to begin again where they left off. The main reason they were discontinued was that financial support for them was withdrawn by the main consuming countries. Some aspects of the design of the agreements were inadequate, however, which made it easier for wealthy countries to find the excuse for closing them down. The world has changed since 1989 but the essential lessons learned by UNCTAD in establishing these agreements should be understood before deciding on the design of a system that would avoid the mistakes of the past and one that would be more in harmony with today's economic and political climate.

Naming the actors

The essential reading on this topic is *Taming Commodity Markets* (1992) by Gamani Corea, the secretary-general of UNCTAD during this period. Considering the book was written a decade ago, Corea displays considerable prescience in stating that 'Supply management by producers, whatever the instrument used, may prove to be a necessity in the light of the prospects for commodity prices over the next decade.'

Corea spells out the purpose of a supply management programme and who, ideally, should implement it.

> The essence of price stabilisation arrangements is supply management, whether through export quotas or stockpiling. Commodity supplies are under control of the producing countries and if they were to succeed in restricting or managing these supplies through agreement among themselves they would be able, unilaterally, to influence prices. This is especially true of export quotas since these do not require actions by consumers.[2]

Corea acknowledges, however, that while producing countries may have the power, in theory, to implement control over their own exports, they may lack the administrative capacity to organise a programme to manage global supplies. He identifies one of the most important difficulties he encountered in forging and maintaining these agreements: 'It would seem also that the developing countries, lacking the organisation and facilities needed to design and foster agreement on price stabilisation schemes, placed unduly heavy reliance on the Secretariat of UNCTAD to help in this task.'[3] For this and other reasons, including the monitoring of imports, Corea concludes that any scheme designed to manage production is best undertaken with the agreement of consuming countries as well as producing countries.

Indeed, supply management could also be said to be in the interests of consuming countries. Another commentator, Sydney Dell, has put it this way:

> While [the] ... opposition [of the industrialised countries] could be understood in terms of their short-term interests, it was less clear that it was rational in the longer run perspective, since rising real income in the developing countries was clearly in harmony with the interests of developed countries from many points of view, including the larger markets for their exports that a prosperous Third World would imply.

We may conclude that a global management supply programme may be easier to implement if consuming countries agreed to assist with its implementation, and that arguments could be found to demonstrate that it was in their own long-term interests to do so.

The inclusion of other actors may also help to bring about a stronger consensus. It should be borne in mind that the UNCTAD-initiated commodity agreements were between states, not representatives of the commodity producers themselves. Some observers consider that this feature of supply management agreements represents a weakness. First, commodity producers have a more direct and urgent interest in maintaining higher prices for the goods they produce. Second, some governments, given their power to allocate export quotas to producers, abused that power by offering quotas to domestic producers whom they favour and denying them to producers whom they perceive to oppose some aspect or other of government policy or on the basis of racial or cultural identity. The system, too, was abused in some cases by corruption.

Individual farmers are likely to respond to the suggestion that they should reduce production capacity as just another 'trick' from the outside world which will impoverish them further. It is very important, therefore, that the substantial benefits likely to arise from a successful supply control programme are explained to them by people they trust – preferably fellow farmers. If they could be sure that cutting production by, say, 5 per cent would double their income, they are likely to cooperate.

In most producing countries there exists at least a semblance of organisation of farmers. These may be farmers' unions, associations of co-operatives and/or associations of producers of a specific commodity. It seems likely that any agreement would be considerably strengthened if these organisations participated actively in the implementation of any future agreements. Clearly, the representation of the interests of farmers differs from one country to another. Moreover, these arrangements may vary from producers of one commodity to those of another. This suggests that a new initiative to manage supply of commodities should identify, and where necessary support, these organisations in each country and enable them to acquire the necessary resources to allocate export quotas among themselves by mutual agreement.

The task of coordinating new thinking on this subject, especially in developed countries, might be strengthened by encouraging the participation of some of the major development NGOs. Several of these organisations have, for many years, identified low commodity prices as a major cause of poverty. They have considerable influence in many forums and could be relied upon to support and lobby for such arrangements.

Bringing the parties together

By far the greatest problem faced by Corea, and by other officials engaged in establishing these kinds of agreement, has been the difficulty of bringing the large number of countries, producers' representatives and other interested parties together. Each of these stakeholders will differ in size and influence. They will be differently established in different markets and have different political leanings and associations. The commodities crisis, however, is so profound that one might assume that the differences between these actors are likely to be insignificant compared with their common need to solve the tropical commodities crisis.

The prelude to previous efforts to bring some order to these markets has, in the past, always been marked by an extreme lack of generosity not only between producing countries and consuming countries but also between the various producing countries themselves – especially in discussions concerning quota allocations. Such quotas are an essential part of any supply management programme. Each country, by mutual agreement, needs to be allowed to export no more than a specific quantity or quota per year of the commodity in question. We should remember, however, that these agreements were eventually established, and worked while they lasted, very much in favour of the producers.

Corea argues that the need for developing countries to act together is essential: 'When commodities are supplied by a large group of countries, none of which has significant market power individually, it is only by collective action that markets could be influenced.' And, acknowledging that the failure of developing countries to work together reduced the effectiveness of the supply management programme, he says: 'The most important shortcoming on the side of the developing countries was, however, their relative failure to co-ordinate their positions and agree among themselves on a decisive plan of action.'[4]

Before the UNCTAD agreements came into force, commodity prices were higher in real terms than they are today. We should not assume, however, that – in spite of the huge incentive producing countries now have to work together to establish supply control systems – agreement will be easy to reach.

Once the broad objectives of an agreement have been established the difficult diplomatic effort needs to get under way to encourage the participation of stakeholders. This process has already begun. I will return to outline this process later in the book.

How the plan might work

The first task is to persuade potential participants that they should, at least in principle, contemplate the establishment of a supply management programme. This will not be possible unless a more detailed plan is put forward on how the programme will work, who should administrate it, what timetable it should work to, what its more detailed objectives are, and how much it will cost.

Gamani Corea was able to organise the establishment of the 1970s' international commodity agreements with only the twenty-five professional staff of the UNCTAD Commodity Division in Geneva – the number of staff that would be considered a small company in the private sector. Some of the apparatus used to represent the interests of the signatories of the agreements remains intact. Institutions like the International Coffee Organisation, and similar organisations, including those representing cocoa, sugar and rubber-producing countries, still help to represent their members' interests. The Common Fund for Commodities, another construct of the agreement, as mentioned before, also functions but only for non-market intrusion work such as supporting sales promotion, quality improvement and futures market risk-management schemes. UNCTAD itself continues to monitor the relationship between commodity markets and economic development. In other words, any new supply management programme would not be starting from scratch. Indeed, the design of these programmes has also been discussed by these and many other bodies in great detail many times in the past.

Corea offers an outline of any such agreement:

> The commonest are schemes for the restriction of production or exports. The regulation of total supplies to world markets would require the allocation of export shares or quotas to individual producing countries, and an agreed basis for determining such shares would need to be established. Moreover, within each country, means would have to be found for distributing that country's quota among its domestic producers and administrating the allocations that have been decided upon.[5]

This was broadly the model used by UNCTAD for its international commodity agreements. The details of each agreement varied but the agreement on coffee came closest to the model. All the major coffee-producing and coffee-consuming countries signed up to the deal. (A few countries, including Eastern European countries, declined the offer to participate.) After a great deal of haggling and the inclusion of certain flexible arrangements, each country was allocated a quota for total exports. These quotas were based on the historical shipments of coffee from each country averaged over a number of years. Each government was required to issue permits or stamps, as they were sometimes called, to exporters, which allowed them to export their proportion of the total quota. Once the quota was filled no further exports were permitted.

Floor and ceiling prices for each type of coffee were set from time to time, as was the total world export quota. These varied according to the state of the market. If the international prices for residual stocks reached or exceeded the ceiling price, the export quota would expand and a proportion of any stocks would be sold on to the market at the ceiling price. If the international market price of residual stocks fell below the floor price, producing countries could stockpile any difference between the amount they could sell at the floor price and their quota allocation. The cost of financing these stocks, known as buffer stocks, was underwritten by a fund made available mostly by producing countries.

Importing member-countries were obliged, under the terms of the agreement, to monitor their imports by examining the certification of the goods, including certificates of origin, and disallow any coffee imported below the agreed floor price. This system allowed the administrators of the agreement to monitor each country's exports and to identify any cheating or smuggling activity.

One serious weakness of the UNCTAD commodity agreements was that they were based on agreed export quotas rather than agreed export capacity. This is known as an export retention scheme and allowed for the funding of surplus stocks. As this funding was advanced primarily from consuming countries, rather than producing countries, it put the power to continue or abandon the programme in the hands of developed countries which could benefit, at least in the short term, by ending the agreement. This they duly did, in the case of coffee, in 1989 by withdrawing from the funding arrangement – known as the economic clauses of the agreement.

The export retention model used in the UNCTAD agreements gave rise to the problem of storing surplus supplies. Apart from the difficulties of raising the necessary finance to keep these stocks, the organisers had to cope with the problem of keeping semi-perishable goods, like cocoa beans, in stores for sometimes several years. As production capacity often exceeded a country's export quota, the retention arrangements also encouraged cheating by member countries and many traders were willing to smuggle surplus coffee out of the country and sell it on the open market, which had the effect of keeping prices down.

A more robust arrangement would involve the destruction of a small proportion of production capacity. This would, of course, imply the added problem of inspecting individual producers' land in order to regulate the cutting down of trees and the planting of crops. It is possible that new satellite imaging technology could be used for this task. It should be borne in mind that cocoa and rubber trees and tea bushes do not come to maturity until five years after planting and that coffee trees take three years before becoming productive, so, in the case of these important crops, inspections would not have to take place very often. Again, where possible, local farmers' associations would need to be responsible for such work.

Some commentators in this field have expressed concern about the word 'destruction' in this context. A superficial understanding of the idea might lead one to believe that any cutting down of trees or rooting up of crops would take away some of the few assets these poor countries have. This process is going on all the time, however. Old, diseased and less productive trees have to be cut down in order to make way for new ones. Crops like sugar and rice are planted and harvested every year. In May 2002, the Sri Lankan government announced a plan to replace one-fifth of the country's coconut trees, which have been damaged by the effects of drought and poor maintenance. Destruction would simply mean a controlled acceleration of this natural process.

Alfred Maizels of Queen Elizabeth House, Oxford University, another leading advocate of supply management, believes that it would be easier to reach agreement between producing countries if a system based on cutting production was introduced:

> A production reduction scheme does have an advantage over export quota, however, in so far as it is based on a uniform percentage cut in current, or recent, levels of production. Since this would leave the relative production levels of various producing countries unchanged it should not give rise to major disputes about market shares – a common difficulty in negotiation on export quotas.[6]

It would be vitally important for any supply management programme to get the message across that the organisers of the programme mean business. Speculators will simply not believe that surplus stocks can be held back indefinitely from the market. If, however, they witness the destruction of the capacity to produce those surplus stocks they will tend to take long positions on the market rather than short positions. In other words, speculators will buy the commodity in advance of production on futures markets rather than sell them. Consumers and traders will build inventories rather than keep them at a minimum level. This will have the desired effect of raising the market price.

The organisers of the programme should, obviously, make every effort to persuade farmers that cutting capacity can only assist them. It might, however, be difficult to persuade every producer of that commodity in every tropical country to reduce their capacity at the same time and to the same extent. For this reason the organisers of the programme might decide that implementation could be speeded up by offering farmers some compensation for destroying a percentage of their production capacity. This would not be a large percentage. As has been mentioned before, the difference between oversupply and a balanced market is typically a few per cent of total production.

The details of how this might be achieved could be decided upon by each producing country. Some farmers' associations may be able to persuade their members to cut production without compensation. Others might use the programme to accelerate the process of getting rid of poor-quality crop varieties. Whatever method is used, each country would be required to demonstrate that it had a supply reduction programme that reduced its export capacity to the agreed export quota level. By doing this it will have entitlement to its share of any central fund which was made available for the compensation of farmers. Clearly, these funds would have to be returned once prices increased, which should ensure that any individual country uses the funds sparingly and only when necessary. (Some countries – Ethiopia and Brazil, in the case of coffee – are major consumers of their main export crops. There should be no intention within the scheme to reduce this consumption. Export quotas should take account of internal consumption.)

It would, of course, take some time to ensure that all member countries had taken steps to control production and exports. It may, therefore, be necessary, both as a practical measure and from the point of view of sending a robust market signal, for some proportion of stocks to be destroyed as the first act of a new supply management programme. This measure is not as drastic as it sounds. Since the deregulation of markets it has been more difficult to control the quality of many commodities and there has been a build-up of large stocks of substandard products. Destroying these stocks will not only help to introduce some rigidity into the market but also improve the reputation of suppliers on quality standards. Clearly, funding will be required to compensate suppliers for the loss of their stocks but some system for recovering this cost could be built into the system once prices increase. The payment of compensation to owners of stock which is subsequently destroyed may not meet with universal approval, however, if those stocks are owned by trading companies. Any compensation they receive will not benefit farmers or the developing countries that are the intended beneficiaries of the scheme.

In order to understand how a new supply management programme could operate successfully, some knowledge of how commodity markets work is essential. Although the differences between the volume of supply and demand represent the most important influence on price movements, sentiment also plays a major role. Traders do not only act as intermediaries between buyers and sellers. They make the bulk of their income by taking a position on the market – they are also speculators. At present they perceive the markets of tropical products as fundamentally weak – mainly because they see no prospect of successful supply management in the foreseeable future. It would be important, therefore, for any new initiative to be supported by organisations with a reputation for integrity and professionalism. The sentiment in a market can be turned instantly if the right signals are given. Such a change would, in itself, lead to a stronger market.

Investing in processing

One component of new agreements might be to include a linkage with investment of the extra revenue in added-value products. Just as the prices of primary commodities have fallen over the last two decades, the prices of products processed from these raw materials – chocolate bars, instant coffee, and so on sold in Western supermarkets – have staged a significant rise. This suggests an obvious development strategy. The processing and packaging of domestically produced raw materials could form the basis of new manufacturing and service industries in developing countries, thus reducing reliance on raw material production. This, after all, is the ultimate goal of all economic development programmes. If developing countries can be allowed to establish new industries, rather than relying on sterile aid programmes, they can truly contribute to the world's economy.

It may be thought advisable, therefore, to build mechanisms into any agreement designed to encourage countries or producers' organisations to retain some of the increased revenue gained from the increased market price of their primary product. This retained revenue could be used for investment in processing the commodity concerned into higher-value, semi- or fully manufactured products.

Where to start?

The designers of supply management programmes might decide not to try to include all affected commodities at once. By proving that such a scheme could work successfully for one product, the administrators of the programme might more easily convince those interested in the markets of other products to embark on a similar programme. By staging programmes in this way initial costs could be reduced. Corea also raises this idea. 'The possibilities in the area of tropical beverages, for example, where demand elasticities are relatively low and production heavily concentrated in developing countries, might be better than in the case of several other commodities.[7]

Enforcing the agreements

Free-riding is an inherent problem associated with all supply management schemes. Let us say that there are ten countries that produce a certain commodity. Nine of them sign up to a deal to cut supplies and raise the price. The tenth producer refuses to join the agreement and continues to produce the same quantity of the product. The tenth producer gets the advantage of the higher market price without having to cut production.

Instigators of supply management programmes need to do their utmost to ensure that the representatives of all producers of a particular commodity sign up to the deal. In the case of the International Coffee Agreement, several consuming countries decided not to join. They were able to buy cheap coffee from producing countries, provided that the coffee was consumed within their borders. Dishonest trading companies then forged false certification and sold the coffee on to countries that were signatories of the agreement at discount prices. A shortage of high-quality arabica coffee, for which some consumers were prepared to pay a premium, gave traders a further incentive to cheat the system. In addition to these problems, some traders smuggled out of countries quantities of coffee which were over and above the quota allowed them under the agreement.

These various forms of cheating weakened agreements in the past but did not render them ineffective. There will always be those unscrupulous operators who will try to find ways to circumvent any agreement. Their activities can be kept to a minimum by building a robust monitoring apparatus into any agreement and applying a penalties and incentive system to ensure that member countries enforce the rules they have signed up to. This reinforces the argument for including consuming countries in any deal, as they are in a good position to check the certification of imports.

It is also important to ensure adequate supplies of any particular sought-after grade of the commodity. This provision needs to be accommodated within the design of the agreement.

Covering the cost

The costs of establishing an agreement to cover just one commodity would not be high – perhaps a few million dollars. Establishing agreements to cover each new commodity would cost less, as much of the same apparatus could be utilised. These are very small sums in relation to the likely reward that such schemes would generate.

Financing, however, is the Achilles heel of supply management agreements. Producing countries have neither the money, nor the skills, nor the communication systems necessary to establish and run supply control programmes. Aid money is strictly allocated and cannot be used for this purpose unless some major funding agency is prepared to offer new funding. The Common Fund for Commodities, certainly, has more than enough resources to cover these costs but is prevented by its UN mandate from doing so, even though its original funds were to be used for exactly this purpose. Consuming countries could, of course, easily afford to finance such programmes. Indeed, in a fair world, it would seem only reasonable that those countries that have saved billions of dollars a year by importing cheap tropical products should be prepared to expend the few million dollars needed to solve the crisis they have caused, or at least acquiesced in. But, as we have seen in the past, any agreement could be considerably weakened if these countries alone controlled the purse strings.

As mentioned above, it may be necessary to offer compensation to the farmers for each bush, tree or crop that they destroy or fail to plant. On the face of it, this looks like an expensive exercise. It should be borne in mind, however, that farmers are currently being paid a pittance for their produce and in some cases less than the costs of transport and packaging.

Cutting production capacity would have a direct effect on the price of the commodity. There is no reason to believe that this process would be viewed by banks and other financial institutions as different from any other money-making scheme. It may be possible, for instance, for the organisers of the programme to issue bonds linked to the supply management programme.

Funds might also be raised by utilising facilities offered by futures markets. The link between reducing production capacity and increasing price will not be a linear relationship as the price would be likely to increase more rapidly as production was cut to the point where supply equalled demand. Such a relationship would be of great interest to traders and speculators. One might envisage the creation of an instrument, akin to a 'call' option on the futures market, in which the premium paid by the speculator would be used in a fund to help cover the cost of the supply management programme. The instrument would give the speculator the option of buying a futures contract of the commodity at the price ruling at the time when the premium was paid – known as the strike price. As the price rose, subsequent purchases of this option would call for a higher premium and a higher price. The deal would need to be underwritten by the owners of the commodity, which could be a government of a producing country or a producers' association.

Another possible way of financing national programmes would be the imposition of an export tax on the commodity in question. The level of tax would have to be coordinated by the signatories of the agreement for all exporting countries. The effect would be to raise the price of the product and deliver a stream of income to governments which could be used to finance the scheme. Such taxes are permitted under WTO rules, but the World Bank and IMF are implacably opposed to such taxes, claiming that they distort markets.

Commodities with a wider growing area

The UNCTAD team found that the characteristics of the market for each commodity were sufficiently different to warrant a variation in the designs for supply management programmes. One of the most obvious differences between the markets is the spread of countries in which the commodity is grown. Coffee, cocoa and coconuts (copra), for instance, can only be grown in the tropics. Cotton is a very important commodity for some of the poorest tropical countries but it can also be grown in sub-tropical and even warm temperate climates. The USA produces a fifth of the world's cotton. US cotton farmers are heavily subsidised by their government at a rate which is five times that received by US grain farmers. (The largest 10 per cent of US cotton farmers receive 75 per cent of cotton subsidies.) Sugar cane is grown most successfully in the tropics but sugar beet can be grown almost anywhere.

It may be that the production of these more widely grown commodities is highly subsidised in wealthy countries, but because developing countries have no monopoly of production any supply arrangement must focus on the removal of production subsidies and import barriers erected by consuming countries.

The markets of tropical commodities vary in many other ways. Some, like tea, are produced mainly in large plantations. Bananas are produced both as a plantation crop and by small-scale farmers. Some crops, like nutmeg, are grown in significant quantities by only two or three countries. Vanilla represents a significant proportion of the exports of a couple of East African countries, but the natural product competes with synthetic vanilla. Some tropical vegetable oils, like palm oil, can be substituted for by temperate oils, such as rapeseed oil. Some commodities are more perishable than others. Some markets are tiny, others massive. Some markets are dominated by a handful of trading companies, while there may be thousands of companies trading others.

More importantly, perhaps, some countries with a very large output of a particular commodity – rubber would be an example

– have mixed economies and, therefore, less overall dependency on that commodity. They may not wish to take the risk of worsening their relationship with the industrialised world by adopting a supply management programme.

For these reasons, each programme will have to take account of the characteristics of the market of the commodity involved. It is very likely that no programme can be devised to help producers of many commodities in this way. The object of the exercise, however, would be to gain the maximum benefit for producers in as many commodities as possible in as short a time as possible. The ultimate objective is to make developing countries less dependent on these products – to offer them the option of using the revenue they derive from their exports for investment in more sophisticated goods.

Flexibility and dynamism

Another criticism of past commodity agreements is that they failed to respond quickly enough to market trends and changes in consumer demand. Large programmes, by their very nature, are often unwieldy. These problems can be overcome, somewhat, by establishing efficient decision-making structures and by properly delegating responsibility. There is no reason why the operators of the scheme shouldn't, from time to time, act as an agent and enter the market to buy and sell the commodity when it was obvious that their preferential and superior knowledge of future supplies would enable them to trade in a way that would benefit producers. They should also be prepared to pass market signals to producers to help them match quality requirements with changing demand.

Conclusion

This outline of a possible model for a supply control programme needs to be refined greatly before it could be implemented. It would, however, serve as a basis of discussions between countries and organisations that have a pressing need to tackle the crisis.

The difficulty of instigating, funding, designing and implementing such programmes should not be exaggerated. The European Union administrates a programme to assist farmers called 'set-aside'. In this scheme European farmers are entitled to abandon farming on a proportion their land and receive a grant for doing so. One objective of this scheme is to allow the abandoned land to 'return to nature' and encourage the natural seeding of wild plants that provide the food and habitat for wild birds, insects and animals that have become threatened in Europe by the loss of habitat to intensive farming. Another objective is to augment the farmers' incomes so that they can stay in business. Whatever the justification for the policy, the cost and administrative complexity of the scheme, which applies to millions of individual farms, is enormous. And this is just one, minor component of the Common Agricultural Policy. Establishing and running a supply management programme for tropical commodities is likely to be far less difficult to administrate than set-aside. We might bear in mind that Gamani Corea was able to organise the establishment of the international commodity agreements with only the 25 professional staff of the UNCTAD Commodity Division.

The outline of the model for supply management programmes would need to include a central administrative secretariat. The activities of this body would need to be controlled by some forum working to an agreed democratic structure and representing the interests of signatories of any agreement. The secretariat would need to work closely with other interested bodies such as the commodity producers' organisations, UNCTAD, and so on. Each producing country would need to set up its own administrative and monitoring structure which would answer to the central secretariat. Clearly, a large number of people would need to be involved, but there is no reason to believe that any more would need to be employed than were employed to run the previous

UNCTAD-instigated programmes which were found to be manageable and cost-effective.

The support for the establishment of a programme to control supplies of tropical commodities has not arisen spontaneously. The growing realisation that no other strategy will offer a solution to the crisis has already been taken up in some countries. In May 2002, Vietnamese coffee traders agreed to withhold up to 300,000 tonnes of coffee from the market. Heaps of low-grade coffee were set on fire in front of a group of journalists in Colombia in June 2002. Many more such actions are likely to occur as long as the crisis lasts. These actions are not going to be effective, however, until they are coordinated worldwide.

Note

1. These are 1980s' levels; the current figure is some US$360 billion. Public Ledger, 18 February 2002.
2. G. Corea, *Taming Commodity Markets*, Manchester University Press, Manchester 1992, p. 186.
3. Ibid., p. 147.
4. Ibid.
5. Ibid.
6. Alfred Maizels et al., *Commodity Supply Management by Producing Countries: A Case Study of Tropical Beverage Crops*, Clarendon Press, Oxford 1997.
7. Corea, *Taming Commodity Markets*, p. 189.

CHAPTER 5

THE BENEFITS OF
SUPPLY MANAGEMENT

Boosting prices

The greatest and most obvious benefit of bringing the supply of a tropical commodity once more into line with demand would be a rise in the market price of the commodity. The degree of the rise would depend on several factors. It would be limited to the level at which it began to discourage demand. This would vary greatly between different commodities.

Some of the vegetable oils produced from tropical crops, such as coconut, groundnut and palm oil, can be substituted with other vegetable oils grown either in the tropics or in other parts of the world. It is common practice among margarine manu-facturers, for instance, to produce their product from a blend of several vegetable oils. This blend changes according to the relative price of each oil. If the price, say, of groundnut oil were to be driven too high by controlling supply too tightly, more corn oil would be used if it remained cheaper. This might also be true of the so-called hard fibres – sisal, jute, hemp, abaca, and so on. These fibres already compete fiercely with polypropylene, a tough thermoplastic, in the manufacture of bags and twine. They also compete with each other in certain uses. Some food flavourings and colourings, such as vanilla, annatto and cochineal also have synthetic substitutes. Many discerning customers are becoming very much more wary of consuming artificial chemicals with the food they eat, however, and the trend has been towards, rather than against, natural food additives.

We must also be aware of the special case of commodities like sugar and cotton that are grown widely in the tropics but are also grown in temperate countries. In such cases the best plan of action is likely to be the abolition of farm subsidies offered in those temperate countries as called for by the WTO. This would, at least, allow tropical farmers to compete on a level playing field with their richer counterparts and would almost certainly lead to higher world prices.

Those charged with the task of designing supply management programmes for these commodities will need to carry out the necessary research and create market models to discover by what degree production should be curtailed to achieve a certain effect on the price and how far a rise in price would affect demand. It may well turn out that very little could be achieved by cutting production in some commodities. The goal should be to apply the correct management of supplies to achieve the maximum and sustainable price rise.

There will be many commodities where supply control will increase prices dramatically. As we have seen, commodities like coffee could rise to many times their existing price without having any effect on demand. The same is likely to be true of many spices, which have sold at considerably higher prices in the recent past without a discernible affect on demand. Historic prices, which were, of course, in most cases much higher than they are now, would be a useful first guide to how high prices could rise when controlled by supply management systems.

Most of the problems of the developing world – political instability, conflict, food insecurity, corruption, the spread of disease, high rates of infant mortality, debt, environmental degradation, ignorance, the brain drain and dependence on the production of raw materials – can be addressed by relieving poverty.

Village life could be transformed with a little extra cash. If farmers had more to spend it would stimulate the growth of local industries and services. It would encourage people, especially the young and industrious, to remain in the countryside and relieve the burden on overcrowded cities. The cultural integrity of family life, which represents the social safety net in most developing countries, would be better preserved. There would be less pressure on parents to have more children if they knew that their existing children would survive. An increase in export revenue would help governments to pay off their debts and increase provision for education and health services, provide clean water and improve the infrastructure of their countries.

In Chapter 1, I discussed possible ways of estimating the order of magnitude of the total increased revenue from the sale of tropical commodities that could be expected if supply control was established. Some of these products are consumed within the developing country that produces them. And, as has been said, some commodities might not lend themselves as well as others to supply control. However, if control measures over production and export of these commodities could raise prices to the level they were in 1980, adjusted for inflation, the total net increase in value would be of an order of magnitude of hundreds of billions of dollars per year over today's levels.

Is this a reasonable projected scale? No doubt there are many econometric models that would give different answers and no supply management system can expect to achieve total efficiency. On the other hand, demand for these goods has increased significantly since 1980 as people in industrialised countries earn more disposable income. As the cost of the raw material is only a small component of the retail price of the goods made from these products, customers are unlikely to reduce consumption even if the price of the raw material rose significantly. Indeed, if customers in 1980 were happy to buy these products at the equivalent of these prices, why should they not continue buying them in 2002?

It seems reasonable to assume that the benefits of supply management are at least likely to exceed the total value of current aid programmes in producing countries.

Targeting increased wealth

It has become fashionable to assert that problems can't be solved by throwing money at them. It is certainly true that many aid programmes are poorly targeted and loosely controlled. Too much aid money is eaten up in the administration of aid projects (and, I must confess, by consultants like me). Another high proportion of aid funds ends up in the Swiss bank accounts of corrupt politicians and government officials and of the foreign private companies supplying equipment and services for aid programmes.

If the price of tropical agricultural products could be raised, most of the extra income would be earned directly by farmers and their families, who represent the majority of the poorest people in developing countries. In other words, the benefits would be automatically targeted at the very people that most aid programmes are designed to assist. With more cash in their pockets, farmers would tend to spend more money on goods and services, thus stimulating local businesses. As these businesses became more profitable, they would pay more tax, thus increasing the stream of revenue to governments. With more money farmers could afford to buy food when their own crops failed, thus reducing the ever-increasing threat of famine in the Third World.

Releasing land for food production

As has been said, a reduction in the production capacity of cash crops need not be large to restore commodity prices to fair and remunerative levels. This capacity reduction might lead to the release of 3, 4 or 5 per cent of arable land. The land used to grow cash crops is often the best land, however. It usually needs to be very fertile and near to a source of water.

Farmers try to maintain their overall income by growing more cash crops as the price of these crops fall. This is, of course, one of the causes of the tropical commodities crisis. This increase in cash crop output has helped to reduce food production to the point where many developing countries have turned from net food exporters to net food importers over the last decade or so. This, in turn, has reduced the availability of food to the poorest people in these countries. The natural instinct for most farmers would be to use any land released from the production of cash crops for food production.

Although the strategy of diversification of crops has been found wanting, there may be a world shortage of some tropical crops, medicinal plants for instance, which could be grown in larger quantities without causing their price to drop significantly. Reducing the production of traditional cash crops might offer an opportunity for some farmers to increase their range of products.

Using price rises wisely

If farmers increase their income they are likely to use a proportion of these funds to invest in their farm. Simple equipment, such as sieves, steel ploughs, manual milling, de-husking and oil-expelling machines, and the use of draught animals and storage silos, can not only increase the value of their products but also save a great deal of hard work. The accumulation of a little cash also releases farmers from the clutches of usurious moneylenders and allows them to postpone the sale of their products in periods when prices are low.

The overall objective for economic development in poor countries is, however, to make them less dependent on the production of raw materials and to stimulate the manufacturing and service sectors of their economies. One obvious way of achieving this goal would be for these countries to develop industries to process their own agricultural raw materials into manufactured or semi-manufactured products. Such development would require the acquisition of a range of different skills. If these added-value products are to be marketed internationally, they would have to be produced to the quality standards demanded by consuming countries. They would need to be attractively and properly packaged. They would also need to be marketed professionally and market-branded where necessary.

The processing of agricultural products in developing countries is likely to be cheaper than it would be in consuming countries, not only because of the easy access to raw materials but also because wage rates are lower in these countries. Certain costs might be higher for some products, however. Transporting boxes containing jars of coffee or honey, for instance, costs more over long distances.

In order to pursue this strategy, processors in developing countries would need to establish training schemes, access to clean water, to buy capital equipment and to acquire a knowledge of marketing techniques. All these elements cost money. If the extra revenue flowing from the export of raw commodities could be ploughed back into the production of added-value products, however, it could help to release these countries from dependency on primary agricultural products.

This process need not start with the production of highly sophisticated processed goods such as boxes of chocolates or ready-to-cook meals. Considerable value can be added to agricultural commodities by proper cleaning, sorting and grading. Packing products in new, standard weight bags can add value. Simple processes such as de-husking, milling and oil extraction can also increase the value considerably. The next level of processing – canning, refining, packaging for retail sale, and so on, could be contemplated if investment derived from the income raised by less sophisticated processing was ploughed back into the business.

An increase in farmers' revenue due to supply management of tropical commodities may not automatically result in increased investment in processing. The benefits of supply management, however, are unlikely to last indefinitely if they are not used wisely. Governments and development agencies need to use the opportunity offered by higher commodity prices to redirect their efforts towards sustainable added-value processing projects. This could be achieved in a number of ways.

The gradual reduction of escalating tariffs for least developed countries (LDCs) through the European 'Everything but Arms' initiative, the US Africa Growth Opportunity Act and similar initiatives made by other consuming countries is likely to stimulate investment by multinational companies, among others, in processing commodities for export. As we have seen, however, the incidence of transfer pricing abuse, tax holiday demands and corruption opportunities means that such investment may not be as valuable as it seems.

Governments and development agencies need also to stimulate local investment by the farmers themselves. Farmers could, for instance, be encouraged to pool some of their extra earnings into savings schemes which could be used to buy storage facilities and the simple equipment needed to add value to their products. Agricultural extension services could be widened to include training on the use of such equipment and on organising collective marketing strategies.

At a national level, laboratories need to be set up to test the quality and hygiene standards of food products, and quality-control systems need to be put in place in food-processing plants. New added-value products could first be test-marketed to local airlines, international-standard hotels and tourist centres. These customers need high-quality, safe products, which at present can only be purchased from abroad. If local suppliers could fulfil their needs, it would save the country a great deal of precious foreign currency and lower the cost of hosting tourists. Once local suppliers are able to satisfy these local consumers that they can be relied upon to deliver goods of the required type and quality, in acceptable packaging, regularly and on time, these suppliers can begin to contemplate export marketing programmes.

Governments also have a role, through their export promotion departments and ministries of trade, not only to inform the outside world of the processed products available from their country but also to put together business plans for individual processing projects to attract potential local and foreign investors. National education programmes should also be established to emphasise the need to reduce dependency on raw materials and to create sustainable processing industries.

Assisting the democratic process

Politicians in Third World countries are more reliant on aid agencies than they are on their rural communities for government revenue. This makes it difficult for them to represent their people through democratic structures. If the countryside, which represents the bulk of the population of these countries, became wealthier, more revenue would flow from both farmers and local businesses in the form of direct and indirect taxes. This change in origin of revenue is likely to require governments to pay more attention to the interests of country people when developing economic and social policy.

In addition, the stimulation of more collective activity among farmers in post-harvest activity and agricultural processing would be likely to give rise to more robust political activity, in which groups of farmers and processors could make more successful representations to government for changes or initiations in policy.

Autonomy

Another important advantage of supply management is that it can be initiated and established by tropical countries themselves. We have discussed at length the arguments for and against the participation of consuming as well as producing countries in supply management programmes. Although it may be found, either for legal or for practical reasons, that consuming countries should be involved in these programmes, the initiative must be made by producers and producing countries. As sovereign nations, they are entitled to manage their production and trade in agricultural products to their advantage.

Developing nations are restricted in many ways from taking action for themselves to improve the lives of their citizens. Their dependency on aid and credit means that they often have to adopt policies which they don't necessarily agree with. Many countries lack the resources to discover whether the policies they are required to adopt by donors will benefit them or not.

The objectives of supply management programmes are unequivocal. They would be designed for the purpose of addressing the tropical commodity price crisis, to relieve poverty, and to save the economies of developing countries from slipping even further behind the rest of the world. They can be designed by developing countries for developing countries.

Unlike aid payments, this revenue would have no strings attached to it by donors. There would be no need to use the money to buy goods from the donor country. There would be no need to cast a vote for motions in international negotiating forums which are not in developing countries' interests. Countries would not be forced to sell off public utilities, such as water supplies. Unlike aid money, also, there would be no need to spend a significant proportion of the revenue on endless conferences, workshops, foreign consultants and monitoring and evaluation studies. As the extra income would accrue directly to farmers in the form of a higher price, there would be also less risk of it being appropriated by corrupt politicians and officials.

An increase in export revenue would certainly reduce some countries' dependency on aid and would also help them to reduce their debt burden. This, in turn, would strengthen their bargaining position in the international community in trade and other negotiations, thus restoring a degree of sovereignty over their own affairs.

Benefits to developed countries

A rise in the price of cash crops would have to be paid by people in consuming countries. This would represent a transfer of resources from rich countries to poor countries. A more prosperous developing world, however, would also bring benefits to industrialised countries. We have seen that one of the objectives of wealthy countries in their neoliberal development programmes is to sell more of their goods to poor countries. In the debate in the US Congress, Senator Richard G. Lugar said that one of the reasons for enacting the Africa Growth Opportunity Act was to assist the USA to compete with the EU in supplying Africa with machinery, electronics, financial services and (believe it or not) agricultural products. He complained that, at present, the USA has less than 10 per cent of the African market.

A poverty-stricken Third World presents salesmen of sophisticated products with a problem akin to sucking blood out of a stone. All that development projects can do for them is to encourage the growth of wealthy elites in poor countries who can afford to buy these products. A more wealthy developing world could afford to buy many more goods from industrialised countries.

The developed world is also acutely concerned about the increasing flow of narcotics into their countries and the growth of crime associated with the drug trade. Drug abuse represents a massive cost to the industrialised world not only in terms of human misery but also in the cost of importation and in enforcing drug laws. Third World farmers don't want to produce narcotics, and often take tremendous risks in doing so. If, however, they are faced with the dilemma of failing to feed their families or growing opium poppies, marijuana or cocaine, they have no choice. Higher tropical commodity prices would go a long way to reducing supplies of these drugs.

Impoverishment in the Third World leads to conflict, which is not confined within developing countries. As we have seen, over the first two years of the twenty-first century, poverty and a sense of injustice and humiliation can provide the conditions which, for some people, provide a justification for terrible acts of terrorism. The relief of poverty and the restoration of autonomy in poor countries may also reduce this resentment and lead to a safer world.

Changing trade rules to fight poverty

Although, in practice, the World Bank and the IMF still coerce developing countries into adopting liberalisation measures, the rhetoric has changed. The term 'structural adjustment' has become so discredited that it has been abandoned in favour of 'poverty reduction' in the title of development programmes. The World Bank and the IMF still maintain that economic liberalisation is the key to poverty reduction, and so, no matter how much they change the wording on the label of their brand of medicine, it still won't cure the patients. Everyone involved in Third World development knows that the World Bank and the IMF will not be easily diverted from pursuing these policies despite all the evidence of their previous failure. It is now the rhetoric that matters, not the substance.

Increasing poverty levels have provoked the many critics of these institutions to call for the abandonment of ideas linking trade with development. They say that only a massive rise in the provision of aid can effectively address the poverty issue. A radical strategy designed to solve the tropical commodities crisis might, paradoxically, make it possible to square these two apparently opposed positions.

To give them the benefit of the doubt, we might imagine that policymakers in the World Bank and the IMF believe that the measures they advocate will work sooner or later but are embarrassed by their lack of progress. Would it be possible to modify their strategies in such a way that they would deliver the equivalent of the massive aid budget that their opponents advocate? Since the economists of the new orthodoxy insist that trade – and not aid – must be the weapon to fight poverty, then why not allow trade to do just that?

As we have seen in Chapter 1, if the volume of exports of tropical commodities could be controlled, then the benefit to the suppliers of those commodities could be in the order of hundreds of billions of dollars a year – enough perhaps to double the income of billions of the poorest people in the world. (Doubling the income of typical Third World farmers would still mean that they earned far less than official poverty rates in most industrialised countries, of course.)

If the final objective of the opponents of the new economic orthodoxy are the same as the stated objectives of the World Bank and the IMF, namely a reduction in poverty, then these opponents should have no objection if this end is achieved through a rationally reorganised trade system. Indeed, as this book has attempted to demonstrate, there are many advantages of using trade rather than aid as the means to address the scourge of poverty. These advantages include the direct targeting of increased revenue towards the rural poor of developing countries, the reduction of overcrowding in the poverty-stricken cities of these same countries, and all the other benefits set out earlier in this chapter. In addition, higher incomes for farmers would restore the dignity of working productively to earn a living wage rather than relying on handouts of bags of rice from the USA and powdered milk from Europe.

Acceptance of this concept would imply a major shift in development thinking in which development and trade are no longer linked in some spurious rationale, dressed up in pseudo-mathematical economic jargon, designed to further the domination of the world's commerce by powerful companies. Trade could be made into a powerful instrument to tackle rural poverty in developing countries. It would mean a reinterpretation of the difference between fair trade and free trade. But, as discussed in Chapter 1, there really is no such thing as free trade; nor are even the most dedicated free marketeers calling for free trade. Commercial and financial institutions could not survive without strict government regulation of, and intervention in, the trading system at many levels. Government bodies, for instance, have to remain responsible for providing rules for trade in an international framework.

The battle to harness trade to the cause of poverty reduction in tropical countries needs to be fought on three fronts:

- Most importantly these countries must control exports of their commodities so that supplies are once more balanced with demand at acceptable price levels.
- Second (as discussed in Chapter 3), the issue of increased market access for some tropical commodities as well as for the goods processed from those commodities is extremely important. Tropical producers of sugar, rice and cotton should be allowed to compete on a level playing field with producers of these products in countries that heavily subsidise their farmers and erect substantial tariff barriers to protect their domestic markets. In addition, barriers erected by consuming countries to deter the importation of processed tropical products should be eliminated.
- Third, agricultural development programmes must no longer concentrate on increasing supplies of cash crops, and in future must focus on the need to enhance the value of existing production by assisting farmers to properly sort, grade and pack their crops, by encouraging collective activity among farmers to achieve economies of scale and by stimulating the processing of their goods into added-value products.

The special merit of this strategy is that it is simple and that it can begin to work almost immediately. Unlike the present aid system, it will not require thousands of different types of projects set up by hundreds of different aid agencies. The WTO is designed to deal with the first two trade elements of this strategy, and the third element only requires agencies to cut, initially, some of their programmes before initiating new, more effective ones.

The scale of the objectives and the simplicity of this strategy will also make it attractive to organisations that campaign on behalf of the world's poor. It can be described easily and the staged progress towards its implementation can be readily followed through publicly accessible meetings of the WTO. Anyone who openly opposes the idea will have to justify their opposition.

Those who support this strategy, however, must recognise that it cannot replace all aid programmes. Many poor countries, particularly those in the semi-arid regions of Central Africa and those blighted by civil war, cannot survive without aid even if the prices of export commodities rise – they simply can't produce enough of them. Indeed, there is a strong moral argument for retaining all existing aid programmes as well as instituting this transformed, trade-based strategy. We must recognise, however, that the generosity of wealthy countries towards the developing world is very limited and if many poor countries can significantly increase their earnings from trade, aid budgets will be cut.

Alfred Maizels also sees the link between supply management and general economic development.

> Negotiations between developing and developed countries should be given high priority with the aim of evolving a viable and coherent set of measures to raise persistently depressed levels of commodity prices and commodity export earnings of developing countries. Such measures could be a key element in a renewed international strategy to accelerate the development process, particularly in low-income commodity-dependent countries.[1]

Those advocating supply management as the principal means for distributing significant resources to poor producers must also be aware that they may be making a historical break with the past and rejecting the unreliable, and at times irrelevant, culture of aid dependency.

Note

1. Sir Alfred Maizels et al., *Commodity Supply Management by Producing Countries: A Case Study of the Tropical Beverage Crops*, Clarendon Press, Oxford 1997.

CHAPTER 6

INTERNATIONAL RULES AFFECTING SUPPLY MANAGEMENT PROGRAMMES

The sovereignty of an individual country is limited by the extent to which it has committed itself to abide by conditions laid down in any of the bilateral, regional and multilateral agreements it has signed or in any agreements it has made with aid donors or creditors. When considering the management of supplies of exported commodities, every country is entitled to act unilaterally to control production and exports. Clearly, in some cases, such action may contravene some aspect of domestic legislation, such as competition policy law, but each country has the right to amend such laws as it thinks fit. Participation by an individual country in an international commodity agreement could, however, be disapproved of by major development organisations such as the Bretton Woods institutions – the World Bank and the IMF. In their negotiations with such bodies, countries often agree to adopt certain domestic policies as a condition for receiving aid and development packages including credits, grants and loans. These could be withdrawn if governments decide to change domestic policies affecting the economy.

It is too early to predict the response of these bodies to supply control schemes. International commodities organisations and major NGOs have had meetings with the World Bank to discuss the use of supply control as a means of addressing the current crisis. The World Bank did not support the idea but has not put forward any details of its preferred solution to the problem. The Bank is, however, only too aware of the implications of the crisis for debt repayment and economic destabilisation. The case for supply management has not yet been fully formed and the campaign to bring commodities into a more central position on the world economic stage has only just begun.

The IMF and the World Bank are wedded to the idea of free-market solutions to development problems even though they are themselves, ironically, part of the public sector. (Bloated salaries and luxurious staff perquisites make these organisations an example of the worst excesses of public-sector waste and extravagance; it would be interesting to find out how the staff of these organisations would react to the suggestion that they should compete with the private sector.) Their opposition, on ideological grounds, will almost certainly prevent them from proposing supply management programmes themselves, but they might find it difficult to oppose such schemes in the face of a coordinated campaign on behalf of the very people that they are mandated to assist.

Supply management may face challenges linked to other international agreements and important trading relationships. When in 1993 the Association of Coffee-Producing Countries (ACPC) resurrected another retention scheme, Mexico, as a member of the NAFTA agreement, with Canada and the USA, faced a legal challenge if it took part.

The position of the USA on supply management is very important, especially as the USA is likely to be the major opponent of any scheme which would have the effect of increasing its import bill. Latin American countries are the main suppliers of tropical commodities to the USA. The relationship between the USA and Latin America has been strained over many decades, often over the issue of agricultural trade. The USA has major commercial agricultural interests in the region. These include fruit plantations and processing plants owned by large US trading companies. The fall in commodity prices, combined with US insistence on freely marketing its own, often heavily subsidised, agricultural produce in the region, has not improved the relationship.

The fall of the coffee price, especially, has had the effect of boosting Latin American cocaine production, which in turn adds to the already appalling levels of drug abuse in the USA. The USA, too, has shown some concern about the spread of 'Castroism' in Latin America, which is likely to gain support as poverty levels rise. It is not inconceivable, therefore, that the USA might be won round to the idea of supply control as a less unpleasant option. In June 2002 Mexico imposed an anti-dumping import duty on imports of subsidised US rice despite its NAFTA agreement not to do so. A more acquiescent response by the USA to this move might indicate an increasing recognition of the difficulties faced by Latin American agriculture.

Most tropical countries are ex-colonies of European nations and many, especially African countries, retain strong trading links with the EU. The group of seventy-one ex-colonies in Africa, the Caribbean and Pacific (ACP) region enjoy special preferential trading access to the EU. This relationship strongly influences these countries' pattern of both trade and production. In order to retain this relationship, now enshrined as the Cotonou Agreement, they are obliged to commit themselves to certain domestic and economic policies. The EU is deeply divided about any moves to reduce protection and subsidies for its farmers. It may prefer supply management, as a way of tackling the tropical commodity crisis, to a reform of its Common Agricultural Policy (CAP).

NAFTA, the Cotonou Agreement and other similar trade agreements between countries need to be taken into account when discussing the legal implications for multilateral supply management projects. They may act to hinder cooperation between countries but, on the other hand, they may represent useful forums to obtain agreement. The Cotonou Agreement, for instance, which combines preferential trade concessions with aid packages, could be used as a vehicle to fund supply management schemes. All these agreements, however, are now subordinate to the WTO and have to comply with the trade rules set down by the WTO. This means that whatever changes or disputes arise from the establishment of supply control measures, they have to comply with WTO rules or be agreed or settled ultimately through the WTO.

In order to pursue the examination of the legal framework in which supply control measures need to work, it is, therefore, first necessary to understand how tropical commodity issues were dealt with in the past and to look more closely at the role and powers of the WTO.

The role of the WTO

In 1948 negotiations were institutionalised in the General Agreement on Tariffs and Trade (GATT), which fixed trading rules between its (mainly developed) member countries and resolved to liberalise trade still further over time. Several rounds of negotiations of trade rules have occurred throughout the history of GATT. The Uruguay Round, which began in 1986, was the eighth and last of the GATT rounds.

In 1961 the United Nations Conference on Trade and Development (UNCTAD) was established, based on the belief at that time that fundamental changes in established trading patterns were needed to improve the economic position of developing countries. It wasn't until April 1974 that the Sixth Special Session of the UN General Assembly approved a Declaration on the Establishment of a New International Economic Order, which would give developing countries control over their own resources. The declaration was received with some hostility by developed countries, and although few of the developing countries' demands on other trade-related issues were to materialise, the International Commodity Agreements (ICAs), discussed elsewhere in this book, were established. In the intervening period, especially since the collapse of the economic clauses of the ICAs, the emphasis in discussions on tropical commodities has been on the reduction of trade barriers.

Prior to the establishment of the WTO, then, there were two relevant UN bodies concerned with negotiations relating to trade in tropical commodities – GATT and UNCTAD. Negotiations on the trade in these commodities were held within GATT by a group specially constituted for this purpose. The GATT tropical products group was constituted to ensure that priority was given to the special circumstances of the poor countries that depended on agriculture and the opportunities and difficulties they might encounter in the removal of tariffs and other trade barriers. There was no agreed definition of the term 'tropical products', and some, like sugar and cotton, that are produced in developed countries were included on the list.

In April 1994, officials from more than a hundred countries gathered in Marrakesh to sign the Uruguay Agreement and to confer the role of further trade reforms on a new body, the World Trade Organisation. The WTO came into being in 1995. Its establishment was the culmination of the long GATT process of international trade negotiations designed to provide agreed rules of trade and to liberalise trading relationships between nations.

Member countries of the WTO (144 as at 1 January 2002) have agreed, in effect, to diminish their individual sovereignty over many areas of commercial and trading activity in return for an agreed system of rules governing trading relationships between members. These rules are established through a nominally democratic process in which all changes have to be agreed by the consensus of all member countries. We will look at the limitations of this mechanism later.

WTO agreements cover many aspects of trade, including intellectual property rights, investment measures, technical barriers to trade, rules of origin, textiles, manufactured products, and so on. The 550 WTO bureaucrats generate mountains of paperwork, often in execrable legalese, covering the proposals, deliberations and findings of dozens of WTO committees and subcommittees. Despite this enormous attention to detail, the language used to record every decision is subject to interpretation.

In the present WTO round of negotiations, no separate group for tropical products has been constituted. All discussions in the WTO on the issue are now lumped together with agricultural issues that affect all countries under the Committee on Agriculture. The discontinuance of the practice of holding negotiations on tropical products in a separate negotiating group was partly influenced by the fact that, by the end of the Uruguay Round, almost all unprocessed tropical products started entering most consuming countries on a duty-free basis.

In the case of commodity agreements, WTO rules (and GATT rules which still apply) have also been interpreted in different ways. For instance, under WTO rules and practice an agreement could be considered as a commodity agreement only where in addition to 'producing countries', those which are 'substantially interested in importation and consumption of the commodity' agree to become its members. Countries which are members of such commodity agreements are permitted, under 'general exceptions' to the provisions of GATT 1994, to impose restrictions on production, imports and exports, even though they may be inconsistent with GATT rules if they are imposed in pursuance of the wider obligations of their GATT agreements (Article XX).

It would seem that under WTO rules consuming countries would have to participate in a commodity agreement but only if the agreement covered the control of exports or imports. Such an agreement would come within the rules, however, if its aim was to restrict production and not exports directly.

Vinod Rege, advisor to the Commonwealth Secretariat on the WTO, has demonstrated this point with examples of what are known, in WTO jargon, as plurilateral agreements. It seems that only producing countries participated in the Agreement on Dairy Products. This agreement was, until its termination in the late 1990s, part of what is now the WTO system. The agreement's aims were to avoid 'disturbances in international trade' by preventing the development of surpluses and shortages and to maintain prices at equitable levels. Its protocols on milk powder, milk fat and cheeses specified minimum export prices. This agreement was listed in the annex of the Marrakesh Agreement (which established the WTO) as a plurilateral agreement, which meant that any member country could choose to become a member if they so wished. The agreement was terminated voluntarily by its members but not because it contravened WTO rules.

The International Coffee Agreement also provides for producing countries, in cases where there is global oversupply, to enter into arrangements aimed at restricting production with a view to bringing balance between supply and demand without necessarily involving consuming countries.

Further evidence in support of the idea that supply management programmes comply with WTO rules comes from Dr Supachi Panitchpakdi, the new director-general of the WTO. He stated in a television interview prior to taking office that,

> the long term solution to the problem that has arisen in international trade in steel can be found only through the adoption by producing countries of an agreement providing staged reduction in production. Such an arrangement could be negotiated under the umbrella of the WTO and supported by the establishment of a World Trust Fund to provide adjustment assistance to industries which would be required to reduce production and to compensate workers who lose their jobs.

The legal basis for supply management programmes is provided by the chapter on Trade and Development of GATT (Part IV), Article XXXVI, which covers 'principles and objectives' for action taken to promote economic development through trade. It states that,

> given the continued dependence of many developing countries on the export of a limited range of primary products, there is need wherever appropriate, to devise measures designed to stabilise and improve conditions of world markets in these products including, in particular, measures designed to attain stable, equitable and remunerative prices thus permitting an expansion of world trade and steady growth of real export earnings of these countries.

Article XXVII on 'joint action' calls on countries to take such action through negotiations and adoption of 'international arrangements'.

A thorough examination of the legal implications vis-à-vis the WTO would need to be undertaken before supply management programmes for tropical commodities could be established under present rules. On the above evidence, however, it seems not only that such programmes are consistent with WTO rules but that the WTO might become the umbrella for introducing them. The procedures for introducing new agreements within the WTO framework are established but will require a great deal of thought on how best to invoke them in the shortest possible time.

It is also possible that some amendments to existing procedures may be necessary to accommodate discussions on the subject. Most previous negotiations in the WTO on commodities have concerned tariff barriers and other restrictions on trade. For this reason, commodities have been lumped together to facilitate the establishment of general rules of trade. It is possible that, given the significant differences between the way an agreement may need to be designed between one commodity and another, the WTO should discuss the subject on a commodity-by-commodity basis. This may require the establishment of yet another sub-committee which could be used for this purpose only.

If, as seems likely, the WTO becomes the obvious forum for negotiating supply management agreements, other relevant organisations, such as UNCTAD and the Common Fund for Commodities (CFC) may be required to adopt an important but subordinate role. The WTO has a limited capacity and understanding of the trade in commodities. UNCTAD and the CFC have had a historical remit through the United Nations to concern themselves with precisely this kind of problem. Like many other organisations, however, including the World Bank itself, the role of UNCTAD and the CFC has been changed over the last few years to reduce their capacity to investigate and intervene in the markets of primary products. It is almost as if there has been a deliberate policy to reduce attention on this subject. Nevertheless, these organisations have an enormous residue of experience in this field and could be used, under the auspices of the WTO and ultimately the United Nations, to carry out the detailed work of designing agreements, administrating them and acting as conduits for funding their work.

Democracy and the WTO

The WTO is housed in a building surrounded by elegant gardens on the shores of Lake Geneva. It was designed to accommodate a large bureaucracy in an age before computers and instant communication systems. The WTO is the hub of international commerce, but the atmosphere inside the building is more like a senior common room. The polyglot staff move confidently through the airy corridors dressed in casual designer clothes. The tear-gas and police batons of the Seattle riots have, like an unpleasant dream, been quickly forgotten. Delegates from developing countries are less confident. They look awkward in these surroundings in their formal three-piece suits or native dress. Strangers in a strange land, they don't know whom to trust.

Officers of the organisation are always on hand to offer advice and information, but the representatives of Third World countries find them unsympathetic. The staff can only repeat the WTO 'line'. They are not in the business of judging the fairness of WTO decisions or helping countries to frame proposals which contradict the official creed.

Unpromising as the organisation may appear, the WTO may be the most likely body to negotiate and initiate commodity agreements, for two main reasons. Since the deliberations of the organisation are closely followed by a wide range of audiences, discussions on the commodity crisis will receive a great deal of publicity. In addition, eventual measures developed within the WTO are likely to be effective because of the consensus nature of its decision-making system. But just how democratic is this system?

The scandal arising from the ignominious breakdown of the WTO ministerial meeting in Seattle in December 1999 highlighted the limitations of the democratic process within the organisation. Developing countries were outraged to find that they were not invited to key decision-making meetings of about thirty powerful countries, the so-called Green Room, which caucused together to make important decisions and ignore Third World interests.

At the next ministerial meeting in Doha in November 2001 many delegates from developing countries reported that industrialised countries threatened the withdrawal of aid, concessionary trade arrangements, and so forth, to force them to vote for proposals that they did not believe were in their interests.

Some key committees, formally linked to the WTO, have no democratic decision-making system. For instance, the WTO's chosen vehicle for setting safety standards on food is the Codex Alimentarius Commission, a joint UN World Health Organisation (WHO) and Food and Agriculture Organisation (FAO) body, set up in 1962. This body sets standards on limits of additives, chemicals and pesticides and other contaminants. Representatives of this organisation include 140 UN member countries but only 7 per cent represent African countries. Developing countries are largely absent from its committees; nevertheless representatives of large transnational corporations including Nestlé, Monsanto, United Brands and Coca-Cola outnumber the representatives of many countries. Existing codes take up twenty-eight volumes of text.

Wealthy industrialised countries are able to maintain permanent missions in Geneva for WTO negotiations and for other regional negotiations. They can afford to employ experienced legal and technical staff to access and analyse relevant information, commission research on areas of interest to them, and lobby effectively through the mass media and at the various relevant forums throughout the world.

Developing countries vary in their ability to marshal the necessary resources to negotiate effectively in trade talks. Many countries are unable to maintain any permanent representation in Geneva.

There is a tremendous imbalance between the resources available to developing countries and those available to industrialised countries. Kenya, Tanzania and Uganda, for instance, have only 2 professional staff in their missions in Geneva while Hong Kong has 10 and the USA has up to 250.

Developing countries miss many activities and negotiations undertaken within the dozens of committees of the WTO. The organisation and its delegate missions generate hundreds of working papers, proposals, research reports and minutes every week. Its rules and modalities would need a small library to accommodate. Yet failure to attend its many committee meetings, often arranged simultaneously, often results in countries voting on proposals which they find later to be totally at odds with their objectives.

Papua New Guinea is a comparatively wealthy developing country but, along with other Pacific countries, it cannot afford to maintain a permanent mission in Geneva. The country's officials say that their negotiators have had to concentrate on Cotonou negotiations. Its participation within the WTO is minimal in that it accepts whatever is decided by others. One official commented that a country 'can only protect its interests if it knows what its interests are and how these can be accommodated within the negotiation agenda'.

A Commonwealth official, commenting on developing countries' lack of negotiating capacity, said that 'The problem is a serious threat to advancing any agreement on trade issues.'

Wealthy countries are clearly embarrassed by the controversy over the lack of democracy within the WTO. Their claims that the consensus system used in the organisation is so much more democratic than the systems adopted in many other UN organisations have been exposed as a myth. In response to the criticism, several industrial countries have provided funding to train Third World negotiators and to help them establish missions in Geneva.

The total funds available for this purpose, however, are far too meagre to provide the capacity for these countries to participate, and therefore influence, WTO deliberations at anything like the level enjoyed by developed countries.

Clearly, any campaign mounted to persuade WTO members of the merits of commodity supply management needs to be prepared to be frustrated by the WTO process. Although delegates of producing countries represent more than half the total membership of the WTO, significantly more assistance needs to be given to help them frame their proposals. The coalition of groups protesting about almost everything the WTO does has grown to be extremely powerful and comparatively well organised. Efforts to steer a programme of commodity control through the WTO might act as a focus for such groups in their campaigning work.

CHAPTER 7

THE TASK BEGINS

The silence surrounding the tropical commodities crisis has at last been broken. In the second half of 2002 several organisations have taken the initiative to analyse the problem and to work out how best to bring it to the attention of a wider public and to press appropriate agencies to find a way to solve the crisis.

Oxfam has, for some time, recognised that the fall in commodity prices is a systemic problem undermining efforts to relieve poverty. It has commissioned studies on several commodities and has decided to launch a campaign on the issue and to discuss the problem with the major development agencies. The Third World Network, the Malaysian-based NGO with a formidable record of analysis and research on development issues, has also pledged itself to publicise the problem and to do what it can to support any action designed to solve it.

There have now been several historically important meetings at the WTO in Geneva, sponsored by the Kenyan ambassador to the WTO, in which representatives of producing countries and of some of the large development agencies and NGOs took part. These meetings have identified the WTO as the appropriate organisation to stimulate practical measures designed to lift commodity prices to an equitable level.

The Oxfam initiative

Oxfam began its campaign by concentrating on coffee producers, who have suffered more deeply and in greater numbers from the crisis than any other tropical farmers. In September 2002 Oxfam launched a campaign on coffee simultaneously in seventeen countries and released their 55-page report on the topic, *Mugged: Poverty in Your Coffee Cup*.[1] The launch received a surprising amount of publicity, including radio programmes on the issue and a number of full-page newspaper reports. This was the most high-profile manifestation of the effort to address the problem to date; as such, we should look at Oxfam's analysis of the crisis and their recommendations for its solution in some detail.

The events leading to the ruination of the international coffee-producing industry are rather complicated but act as a highly illustrative vignette of the entire tropical commodity crisis. Oxfam's approach seems to be a little overwhelmed by the complexity of the problem and presents a rather confused picture of both the root causes of the problem and its possible solution. The report begins with a slightly ambiguous message. It states that 'the crisis is a test of whether globalisation can be made to work for poor people', yet throughout the report we never learn whether this test is likely to be met or not. Oxfam's analysis seems to revolve around whether coffee producing can be made profitable or not. It maintains that coffee now sells for less than the costs involved in producing it.

Almost 80 per cent of coffee is produced by smallholders who don't think in terms of profit. All they know is that they have some coffee trees on the land they work, and that they get less each year from the local trader for the coffee cherries they harvest. They have no option other than to grow coffee, however low the price falls. Profits and costs are the way that coffee plantation owners or large co-operatives think about their business. Oxfam doesn't answer the obvious question it raises when making this point. If all that mattered was the costs and the profit, why would anyone have continued growing coffee over the last decade if the costs exceeded the sale price? The market would surely have balanced itself by now, as 'unprofitable' growers decided to cultivate something else.

The report refers to the World Bank's and the IMF's policies which have encouraged overproduction of coffee in developing countries, but judges these policies, as a cause of overproduction, alongside their inevitable effects. Vietnam is singled out as a major contributor to the problem for increasing its production from 1.5 million (60 kg) bags to 15 million bags in the last decade – as if Vietnam's actions can be considered in isolation from the liberalised economic policies it has been coerced into adopting as the price of joining the world's mainstream economic system.

Currency devaluation is also identified as a cause of the problem, even though devaluation was a key component of structural adjustment programmes. The report also refers to the severe frost in Brazil which severely damaged an entire harvest. The frost caused a sharp price increase to over US$2 per pound for a brief period between the end of 1994 and the early part of 1995. This temporary price hike, Oxfam believes, could also have encouraged subsequent overproduction. Quite why coffee farmers should continue growing too much coffee eight years later, when the price had fallen to 47 US cents a pound, isn't explained. (The 1994 Brazilian frost, incidentally, proves, if proof were needed, that a cut in production can cause a significant price rise.)

Increased output is also attributed by Oxfam to more efficient production techniques in some coffee-growing areas without explaining who sponsored the adoption of these innovations.

The failure of the report to identify the root cause of overproduction is matched by its confusion over the recommendations it makes to address the problem. Overall, it attaches great importance to the International Coffee Organisation's quality improvement plan (more of that later). The report also castigates the major development agencies' failure to invest more in the rural areas of developing countries. Otherwise it calls for additional debt relief for poor countries, the destruction of surplus stocks and a high-level conference involving the World Bank. Other recommendations include the usual raft of ideas that have failed to make any impression on the problem: fair trade, niche marketing, diversification, import tariff reduction, and so on. The report also makes the reasonable request for migrant and seasonal workers to be afforded their rights under International Labour Organisation treaties.

The oddest set of recommendations are directed at supermarkets, giant coffee processors and distributors, asking them to 'pay a decent price to farmers' and to buy increased volumes of coffee under fair-trade conditions. A vague reference is also made to supply management and the need for producers to develop added-value coffee products. The report states that

- Producer and consumer country governments should establish mechanisms to correct the imbalance in supply and demand to ensure reasonable prices to producers. Farmers should be adequately represented in such schemes.
- Producer governments should cooperate to stop more commodities from entering the market than can be sold.
- Producer countries should be supported to capture more of the value of their commodity products.

In its leader the day after the Oxfam coffee campaign was launched, the *Guardian* summed up the coffee crisis and was less equivocal concerning supply management:

Western countries are unashamedly hypocritical. They happily tolerate cartels and restrictive practices when their own products are affected (like agriculture and oil) but abandon developing countries to the worst excesses of market forces when the products happen to be produced only in tropical, not temperate zones.

The leader went on:

It will take a raft of measures to cure the problem, including getting rid of the huge stockpile of unsold coffee that has been built up. But it will also need the revival of an effective, but benevolent, price cartel of the kind that OPEC has latterly become. The industry used to have the international coffee agreement, but it was washed away during a period of excessive liberalisation from which developing countries are still suffering. Such a cartel would, of course, need rigorous monitoring. This should ensure that the benefits go not to the multinationals but to the growers, and that they, in turn, take steps to rationalise in order to create an industry that can survive and prosper.[2]

The Oxfam report was also commented on by Rob Jenkins, Professor of Political Science at Birkbeck College, University of London. In his article, he criticised Oxfam for failing to analyse the consequence of 'free trade' in this context. He described Oxfam as being a vocal advocate of free trade and said that it agreed with Horst Kohler of the IMF that protectionism in industrial countries is the core problem in the fight against poverty. He said that 'in their zeal to expose the double standards (of wealthy countries) critics of Western protectionism have embraced a rather extreme faith in the power of free markets to cure the ills of poor farmers in Asia, Africa and Latin America'. 'Oxfam', he continues, 'admits that coffee farmers in the developing world face neither western trade barriers not producer subsidies. What it will not admit is the logical implication of this. The lesson Oxfam should be drawing is that even when markets in rich countries are not closed, farmers in developing countries suffer anyway.'[3]

In spite of the criticisms of the Oxfam campaign, it has produced some positive results. The Spanish government, with its strong ties to Latin American countries, has passed a resolution supporting the campaign and calling for the World Bank and IMF to support the International Coffee Organisation's plans for cutting the proportion of low-quality coffee produced each year. The Dutch government also made a statement in support of Oxfam's efforts. The British government, true to form, opted for the 'consumer choice' response and offered to make fair-trade coffee available in government offices, thus ensuring that it wouldn't have to spend its own money.

Oxfam has now formed an alliance with forty other organisations – mostly Third World coffee producers' associations and
development NGOs – to press for the report's recommendations
to be enacted.

Coffee: the best candidate

The International Coffee Organisation's (ICO) plan is referred to
in the Oxfam report. The ICO represents 31 coffee producing
countries, and 14 consuming countries are also members (the
ICO is currently trying to persuade the USA to rejoin). Since
the loss of the organisation's ability to control coffee exports under
the International Coffee Agreement, the ICO is mainly concerned with promoting the product and coordinating efforts to
tackle coffee tree pests and diseases. It is involved in fifteen
projects, costing US$60 million, to improve yields and quality.
Most of these are financed by the Common Fund for Commodities. They include a US$6.8 million project in Nicaragua, a US$8.5
million coffee rehabilitation project in Angola, and another project
to improve the quality of robusta coffee in Côte d'Ivoire. Most of
these projects add to the problem of overproduction.

In the spring of 2002 the organisation launched the ICO Coffee
Quality Improvement Scheme as their response to the coffee price
crisis. If the scheme were implemented in full, it could remove
between 3 and 5 per cent of all coffee produced. The scheme aims
to stop the export of coffee that falls below a certain quality
standard. Countries and individual producers not yet able to produce high-quality beans are to be assisted to do so, and money is
being sought to fund this programme. In addition, the ICO wants
to see 5 million bags of low-quality coffee stocks destroyed. Again,
funds will have to be made available to compensate the owners of
these stocks – some of which are wealthy coffee traders. This
move, the ICO calculates, would increase today's coffee price by
20 per cent, or about 10 US cents a pound, and net an extra
revenue for coffee farmers of about US$700–800 million a year.

There is a better market for high-quality coffee than for low-quality coffee, although raising the quality standard usually involves a lot of extra work. The ICO scheme depends on finding the money to implement it. The scheme therefore suffers from the same weakness as the old UNCTAD commodity agreements, in that its operation will effectively be controlled by wealthy funding organisations. There is some indication that some industrialised countries and the large development organisations might be ready to contribute. The scheme is not expected to boost prices to anything like their level twenty years ago, however, and it is hard to see how millions of small-scale producers will be able to improve the quality of their product in a reasonably short time period. In the war against low commodity prices, victory in a small battle may be useful. The ICO's initiative has at least forced the major development agencies to consider the problem.

Managing coffee supplies

In prosperous parts of the world every high street now boasts an elegant coffee shop. A cup of coffee from a Starbucks coffee shop, one of several international chains, costs about US$1.50. Out of this US$1.50, the coffee grower receives just 2 cents. Few denizens of these modern temples of discernment and good taste spare a thought for the people who grow the coffee they are drinking.

The coffee market is one of the largest tropical commodities markets and has been hit hardest by the crisis. The market also has several other features that have led development campaigners to suggest that the coffee market should be the first and obvious candidate for a radical programme of supply control.

Coffee production

Coffee is the fruit of a small tree standing about 20 feet high. The coffee bean is the seed of the cherry-like fruit of the tree. The soft pulp of the fruit and a parchment-like skin around the bean must be removed to obtain the familiar green coffee bean. The beans must then be dried in the sun, and, to improve the overall quality of the coffee, all the unripe, broken and rotten beans (known as stinkers) must be laboriously picked out of the crop by hand. The beans are then packed into 60 kg jute or sisal bags ready for sale.

There are two main species of coffee: arabica, the most widely grown type; and robusta, which is more resistant to disease but has a poorer flavour than arabica and sells at a lower price. Coffee trees are especially vulnerable to frost damage: an entire crop can be wiped out by frost in the short flowering season.

About 6 million tonnes of coffee are produced each year in sixty tropical countries. Around 25 million people are engaged in coffee production. Almost 80 per cent of coffee is produced by small-scale farmers. The balance is produced by co-operatives and commercial plantations of various sizes. Plantation workers are as badly affected by the falling price of coffee as smallholders. According to a 2002 World Bank report, some 400,000 temporary coffee workers and 200,000 permanent workers in Central America have recently lost their jobs.

The taste of coffee depends on how high the trees are grown above sea level, the soils in which they are grown, the number of defective beans in the mix, and the degree to which the beans have been roasted. Most of the major coffee brands are a blend of arabica and robusta and of different quality and roasts. The commercial production of 'instant' or soluble coffee, especially the more popular freeze-dried coffee, involves a highly technical procedure using very expensive equipment.

Unlike some tropical commodities, most people are familiar with coffee as a product. They often have strong preferences for particular brands and know the few companies that dominate the industry – just five companies purchase over 50 per cent of beans for further processing. This familiarity might make it easier for coffee producers to exert some leverage on the industry to accept reform and to inform customers of the depth of the crisis.

The history of coffee prices

In 1977, when the International Coffee Agreement was in operation, the price of green arabica coffee beans reached US$2.23 per pound and remained at an average of US$1.50 between 1976 and 1986. In the 1990s the price averaged just over US$1 a pound; in 2002 the price was approximately 50 cents a pound. Prices are predicted to fall further in the foreseeable future despite an increase in world demand.

Meanwhile, since 1980 the retail price of a jar of instant coffee in the UK has more than doubled. In other words, while the price of green coffee beans has been falling sharply, the retail price of coffee products has been rising. The value of raw coffee beans today is only about one-seventh of the value twenty years ago in terms of international spending power.

The fall in coffee price has been devastating for individual farmers but equally disastrous for countries that rely on coffee for export revenue. The terms of trade of Ethiopia, Burundi and Uganda fell by 30 per cent in just one year, 2000, due to the fall in the coffee price, which has of course fallen further since then.

The price fall hasn't been caused by a collapse in demand. There has been an increase in demand for coffee over recent years of 1.5 per cent per annum. The problem is oversupply. Supplies have increased by 3.6 per cent per year. In other words, the degree of oversupply is not large. A cut in supply of little over 2 per cent would eventually bring the market back into balance and substantially increase coffee prices. But this is the way primary commodity markets work: even a small oversupply has a massive negative effect on prices.

It would be wrong to suggest that all the difference in price between raw beans and the processed product has accumulated as profit to the large multinational companies who dominate the trading and processing of coffee, although this is certainly a significant factor. Most of the difference is taken up with the increasing cost of advertising, branding, packaging and retailing which appeals to increasingly discerning customers in developed countries. All these components of the retail price are accrued in the consuming countries, however.

The accelerating difference between the raw and the retail price suggests an obvious strategy. Coffee-producing countries should brand and package their own coffee and sell it directly to Western supermarkets. Achieving this objective would require a great deal of effort on the part of coffee producers. Developing countries would face the problem of accelerating tariffs. Many processed coffee products are subject to a high tariff wall around the main consuming markets. With the advent of the Everything But Arms initiative and similar initiatives by other developed countries, however, the least developed countries (LDCs) may be able to attract investment in processing plants. Such opportunities are not available to developing countries, however.

Coffee-producing countries would also have to attract significant investment from the very few companies with expertise in coffee processing. Such companies are likely to be reluctant to encourage new competitors. The provision of a hygienic environment and clean water might also present problems. In short, the construction of processing plant is likely to be expensive.

Apart from these difficulties, developed countries would also have to compete in the processed coffee market with their own customers (in developed countries), who are themselves major exporters of coffee products, selling under established brands such as Nestlé and Maxwell House. The USA imports about 24.5 million bags of coffee beans each year but exports the equivalent of 2.4 million bags, half of which are in the form of roasted or soluble coffee. The EU imports 46 million bags, and re-exports the equivalent of 13 million bags – again half roasted or soluble.

Unless the price of raw coffee is raised substantially, coffee-producing countries are unlikely to find the necessary resources to produce their own processed coffee products successfully. Such investment can only come from the additional revenue from raw coffee sales.

Tackling oversupply

The supply management programme of the International Coffee
Agreement collapsed in 1989. In 1993 the Association of Coffee-
Producing Countries (ACPC) initiated the next coffee export
retention scheme, but it collapsed in 2000. The failure of these
schemes to reduce oversupply has encouraged orthodox market
economists to dismiss the whole idea of market management.
Most observers have concluded, however, that unless some control
over supply is once more exercised coffee producers will remain
in penury. To combat the weaknesses of these previous supply
control programmes, production supply capacity would have to
be reduced. That is, trees would need to be cut down.

Of course, different coffee trees vary in productivity, and their
productivity changes as the tree matures. Governments involved
in a supply management programme are likely, therefore, to prefer
to uproot old, damaged and poor-quality trees. They are also
unlikely to be opposed to the destruction of old or damaged
stocks of coffee beans. Although all farmers are likely to benefit
greatly in the medium term from world supply reduction, some
incentive would have to be offered in the form of compensation
to these farmers and stock owners. Very many trees have little or
no value at 2002 prices, so compensation levels may not have to
be high. Any scheme may also need to take account of the difficulties faced by countries where production has been destroyed
by recent conflict.

Every major coffee-producing country maintains a government
agency which still plays some role in the review or regulation of
coffee production and/or exports. Since the liberalisation of the
coffee marketing system in most of these countries, state-controlled
coffee marketing boards play a much diminished role, however. In
Uganda and Ethiopia, for instance, these organisations still exist
but their function of representing coffee producers has been
mainly taken over by private-sector producers and exporters'
associations. Government agencies are, however, still charged with

the task of representing coffee producers' interests at the international level.

It seems obvious that any new supply management programme should be designed and administrated by the existing apparatus that represents coffee-producing countries – the International Coffee Organisation and the Association of Coffee Producing Countries, supported by UNCTAD and the Common Fund for Commodities. The ICO is much diminished in influence after liberalisation, but it still retains a wealth of knowledge and experience in the coffee market. Clearly, these organisations would need support for a secretariat and experts to enable them to administer and regulate a supply management programme at the international level.

The WTO initiative

In April 2002 the Kenyan ambassador to the UN in Geneva, Amina Mohammed, sponsored a meeting at the WTO of the Geneva representatives of other developing countries to discuss the tropical commodity crisis. These participants are required to represent their countries' interests at the many UN bodies based in Geneva and often have no time to consider every issue in detail. After the meeting, however, the representatives were sufficiently disturbed by the sheer magnitude of the crisis that they resolved to commission a further study of the problem and to organise another meeting of experts in the field to investigate the possibility of taking measures within the WTO to address it.

This second meeting of developing-country UN delegates and representatives of UN agencies and NGOs was held at the WTO in July 2002. The study commissioned for discussion at this meeting covered the background to UN agency involvement in tropical commodity markets and the legal status of such interventions. The results of this study demonstrate that, given certain caveats, supply management programmes for tropical commodities appear to comply with WTO rules. In view of this finding and the reduction in the role UNCTAD now plays in establishing rules of trade in these commodities, the July 2002 meeting identified the WTO as the appropriate organisation to stimulate practical measures designed to lift commodity prices to an equitable level. The meeting ended with a resolution to draft a proposal to the appropriate WTO committee to initiate a process leading to the adoption of such measures.

The drafting process had not been finalised before the completion of work on this book but no fundamental changes are likely to be made to the proposal before submission to the WTO Committee on Trade and Development in the first weeks of 2003. It should be borne in mind that the wording of the proposal is the result of meetings between many UN representatives of producing countries and experts, including myself, on trade in tropical commodities. As such, the document offers a fascinating insight into the earliest stages of the process in which ideas within these international trade forums gradually become transformed into resolutions and finally into legislation. It also offers some indication of the priorities of individual countries in their approach to finding ways to resolve the commodities crisis.

Documents drawn up by committees often lack clarity and refinement, however, and this proposal is no exception. The group which drafted the proposal have the unenviable experience of interminable negotiations involving compromise at every level. For this reason, perhaps, the document may be said to lack a degree of resolve and urgency.

Some of the suggestions, such as crop diversification, risk management and quality controls are included for debate. The reintroduction of a role for state-controlled marketing boards is also given some priority. The difficulty of establishing supply control mechanisms is also emphasised and regarded as a 'long-term' solution. This proposal also suggests that consuming countries and multinational trading companies should play a role in efforts to solve the crisis. Reflecting, perhaps, a culture among developing countries of reliance on outside assistance, the proposal also implies that funding from international agencies will be necessary. More importantly, perhaps, a suggestion is made that commodity agreements be 'recommendatory' and that export taxes might be used as an interim measure.

The document is of great historical significance, however, because, for the first time in two decades, it puts the issue of the commodity crisis on the agenda of one of the most important trade negotiating forums and makes a clear and radical recommendation for supply management.

The document emphasises that its suggestions have been listed 'only with a view to providing basis for further discussions and examination. They should not be treated as constituting proposals for action by countries sponsoring the paper.' The proposal calls for the establishment of another WTO committee to examine many aspects of the tropical commodities crisis. Participation in the work of this committee, it says, should be open to UNCTAD, international commodity organisations, the Common Fund for Commodities, the FAO, the Commonwealth Secretariat and other international trade organisations working on commodity problems, and to the international financial institutions. With its mandate for work in the area of commodities, UNCTAD should have special responsibility for providing technical support to the work of the committee and for participation in its work.

Almost all the issues raised in the document are discussed at greater length elsewhere in this book. This proposal, however, represents the most important advance in the effort to put tropical commodity markets under the control of the producers of these products, and for that reason it is necessary to include the essential elements of the document in this chapter.

The preamble to the proposal calls for

urgent action in WTO to deal with the crisis situation created by the declining prices of primary commodities to the trade and development of developing countries which are heavily dependent on their exports.

In an overview of the crisis created by declining prices of primary commodities, this first section of the document states:

> There is an intimate relationship between world market prices and poverty levels. What is perhaps more disturbing is that this trend towards decline in prices is expected to continue and not to reverse in the foreseeable future.
>
> The decline in prices of commodities has also resulted in a steep fall in foreign exchange earnings of countries which are dependent on them for high proportion of their exports. These reductions in total exports earnings have adversely affected the capacity of these countries to import oil, technology and agricultural inputs needed for economic development.
>
> The worst affected are the heavily indebted countries, which are finding that, as a result of decline in their total export earnings, major portion of the foreign exchange revenue goes towards meeting their debt service and payment obligations.

The next section of the document describes the main reasons for decline in prices

- Firstly, poor farmers try to produce more, when prices are falling, in order to maintain the same level of income as they have no other source of income. Increased production however results in depressing prices further.
- What is ironical is that advice to diversify and increase production of these commodities was given to these countries by the World Bank and the IMF, without taking into account the fact that resulting increased productions could, unless world demand increased, depress world prices. The donor countries have also often encouraged and assisted developing countries to undertake cultivation of new agricultural crops, without making adequate study of whether in the long term the world market would be able to absorb the increased production, without depressing prices.
- Thirdly, the domestic and export subsidies that are granted by some of the developed countries for primary commodities also result in depressing the prices of these commodities in international markets. The European Union for instance disposes annually about 5 million tonnes of subsidized sugar in international markets.

The demise of International Commodity Agreements and state-controlled marketing boards are also offered as a causes for the price collapse.

Efforts made in the past, to secure equilibrium between demand and supply, by international commodity organisations have not met with success. The economic clauses in the International Coffee, Cocoa and Sugar Agreements, which permit the concerned organisation to intervene in the market and purchase through their buffer stock management agency have been suspended. However, even if the economic clauses were to be revived, it is doubtful whether in the present market situations buffer stocks operations could be effective in stabilizing prices at levels that are remunerative to producers.

Problems encountered by countries exporting primary commodities as a result of the prevailing almost ruinous low world market prices have been further accentuated by the insistence of the IMF and the World Bank under their structural adjustment programmes that the developing countries receiving assistance under such programmes must liberalize their internal markets by abolishing marketing boards. It is no doubt true that the boards were used by governments to raise revenue in a non-transparent manner, often resulting in a high level of taxation of agricultural producers. At the same time, they provided valuable services to the farmers.

The abolition of marketing boards has resulted in the discontinuation not only of systems for guaranteeing minimum prices to farmers but also of the services provided by them for assisting farmers to enhance productivity and to ensure adequate quality standards.

The concentration of buying power in the hands of a few dominant corporate buyers enables them to dictate, in the absence of government guaranteed minimum prices, the price which they are willing to pay to the poor farmers.

At the end of this section, the document refers to problems of market access into consuming countries.

It is generally believed that one of the reasons, which has so far discouraged foreign multinationals in establishing plants for further processing of the commodities where they are produced, is the existence of tariff escalation, in the tariff schedules of developed countries. As no duties are levied in raw commodities which are used in the processing, the level of effective protection available to the processing industry is much higher than indicated by the nominal rates of tariffs.

The second section of the proposal suggests some 'tentative' ideas for solving the crisis.

Various suggestions are being made by commodity experts and other analysis on the type of action that could be taken in the 'long and short term' at national and international levels, to find solutions to the serious problems, mentioned above, that are encountered by commodity exporting countries.

There is a growing view that the long term solution to the problem posed by 'declining prices' could be found only by 'producing countries' entering into arrangements for management of world supply, through measures involving control over production at national level. In order to avoid unnecessary duplication of efforts, such arrangements may have to be negotiated and adopted, for commodities like coffee, cocoa and sugar, for which international commodity agreements exist at present under their umbrella. In this context it is relevant to note that International Coffee Agreements have provisions which authorize the producing countries to enter into complementary arrangement for management of supplies.

Even though such arrangements would be negotiated at intergovernmental level, they would have to provide for active participation of 'national producers associations' for administrating the supply management programme at national level. Their involvement could ensure greater cooperation by producers in implementing measures involving control over production, which may in the immediate period lead to reductions in their income.

Successful operation of such producers' arrangements would, however, be possible if there was willingness on the part of consuming countries to cooperate. Therefore even though these countries would not be involved, as in the case of commodity agreements, in the decision-making process, they would have to be associated with the work under the arrangements in a consultative capacity. It would also be necessary to establish under the arrangement mechanisms for periodic consultation with private sector companies, involved in buying commodities covered by the arrangements, for further processing and for use in the manufacture of food products.

While in the case of agricultural commodities like coffee and cocoa, producing countries are mainly the developing countries, in the case of commodities like sugar and cotton, a number of developed countries are also significant producers of such products. For these commodities, producers' arrangements would only be viable and effective in stabilizing prices if the developed producing countries also agreed to participate in the arrangements.

It was felt that for commodities like coffee it may be possible to bring supply and demand into equilibrium, if stocks either in producing or in consuming countries were destroyed. As these stocks were held by private-sector agencies, it would however be necessary to buy them. At the prevailing low prices, the cost of buying stocks is not likely to be large while the long-term benefits for the producing countries, resulting from increased prices following liquidation of stocks, are likely to be significant. Assuming there was support for the idea and also political will on the part of developed countries, it may be possible to get the modest financial resources required for this purpose from the international financial institutions. It may also be worthwhile to find out if some part of resources earmarked under the Cotonou Agreement for compensating ACP countries for decline in their export earnings from primary commodities could be utilized for this purpose.

The more difficult question which would have to be addressed was, however, that of equity. Although small farmers might benefit from higher prices, the major beneficiaries of the implementation of the proposal would be trading companies which are holding the stocks and from whom commodities would have to be bought for destruction, and not the poor farmers. Moreover, if stocks held in consuming countries were bought for destruction, the money paid would go to provide windfall profits to the big companies in these rich countries. Such profits may provide incentives to these companies to build up stocks again, as the oversupply is structural in nature.

The second alternative or complementary course of action in the case of coffee and cocoa would be to require farmers to reduce production [by cutting trees]. The government of countries where a large proportion of the farming community is dependent on cocoa and coffee production may find resort to such a course of action highly risky from the sociological and political point of view. Past experience has shown that such programmes can succeed, only if there is support for such drastic measures from all stakeholders and major political parties and if financial resources, required for compensating farmers who are required to reduce production and therefore lose income, in the immediate period following the reduction of production, are guaranteed by the international financial institutions.

Moreover any such course of action, to be effective and successful, would also require simultaneous action by all producing countries to reduce production. Reaching agreement on how far each country should reduce its production is not going to be easy, however, and the negotiations undertaken for this purpose may take years to complete. For instance countries which have been traditional producers of coffee or cocoa may argue that the main responsibility for reducing production should fall on countries which have started production later. This view is not likely to be shared by the latter countries.

One of the ways in which such problems could be resolved is by negotiating arrangements which impose obligations on producing countries that are 'recommendatory'. Under this proposal, producing countries would be required to indicate on a voluntary basis the extent to which they were willing to reduce production within a specified period of time. Incentives for securing compliance could be provided by international financial institutions by guaranteeing to such countries resources for payment of subsidies to farmers who are required to reduce production, to compensate them for loss of income and, where appropriate, for diversification of production to other agricultural crops.

It has to be recognized, however, that any such arrangement, if it is to have significant impact on reducing the chronic structural over-supply that has developed in world markets in commodities like coffee, would require simultaneous action being taken for reduction in production by countries which accounted for a sizeable proportion of world production. Unless a critical mass of such countries show willingness to accept obligations to reduce production on a voluntary basis, and some mechanism is established for surveillance of compliance, the arrangement may not succeed in having any significant positive impact on total availability and price.

The feasibility, from the practical point of view, of administering any such programme for reducing production by requiring farmers to cut trees, and of the costs involved in implementing it, would need careful examination.

How in this situation would the programme for reduction in production be implemented at national level? Some of the farms producing coffee are, for instance, extremely small and have no more than thirty trees. Assuming that, under the proposed arrangement, a member country has agreed to reduce its production by 20 per cent, how should the programme apply the cuts? Should it apply them to all farmers on an equal basis, or exempt small farmers and require only medium- and large-sized farms to cut production?

The farmers who are required to reduce production of coffee or cocoa would have to be further assisted in diversifying and shifting to production of other agricultural products. It would therefore be necessary for each country to examine which new alternative agricultural crops it should request its farmers to cultivate. It would be necessary to avoid taking hasty decisions, as the past experience of countries in trying to diversify reveals very few success stories. Before resorting to any such programme for cutting trees producing coffee or cocoa, the environmental implications of such actions would also have to be carefully examined.

The task of administering any such programme would involve planning and require considerable financial and manpower resources. Most of the countries may also need technical assistance from international agencies for planning and executing such programmes.

Another technique that could be used for reducing production is for producing countries to agree on prohibiting production and exports of low-quality or low-grade commodities. Such measures, it is considered, would be consistent with the provisions of the GATT and the provisions of the Agreement on Technical Barriers to Trade. Some of the developed countries also appear to have adopted measures to prohibit exports of low-grade agricultural products, particularly of fresh vegetables and fruits, in order to ensure higher returns to the farmers for their exports and to establish a reputation for the quality of the exported products.

While such measures were steps in the right direction, they may not have significant impact in the immediate period on the level of supplies available for exports on a worldwide basis and thus would have only a marginal, if any, impact on level of prices.

In the short term, it may be possible for countries to use 'export taxes' to reduce fluctuations and volatility in the prices of commodities and for stabilisation of their export earnings. Any such measure to be successful would, however, require an undertaking by all producing countries to use such taxes and to maintain a certain agreed 'floor tax inclusive export price' on the basis of which international purchase and sales transaction can take place.

The third section of the proposal explains why the WTO should give priority to this issue.

There would appear to be two reasons why it would be necessary to address, in the ongoing work and negotiations in the WTO, the problems posed to the trade and development of developing countries by declining prices of primary commodities. First, as all countries attach political importance to the role of the WTO, raising for discussion in that organisation the 'crisis situation' created by declining commodity prices may bring to the attention of the general public both the need and the urgency of taking early action at international level. Second, and more importantly, this would facilitate solutions being found on the basis of the WTO's rule-based system in the negotiations that are at present being held for the liberalisation of trade in the agricultural sector.

This section goes on to offer an 'illustrative list of elements' that need to be considered within a work programme for the new committee and topics that should be reviewed and examined before being included in this programme. Again, this list includes issues that reflect the concern that some developing countries have about trade which are somewhat peripheral to the crisis. They include for priority consideration for the work programme:

- Further reductions in tariffs by all countries, including tariff escalations.
- Ensuring that such reductions in tariffs by preference granting developed countries do not result in the disruption of trade of the preference receiving countries.
- Provision of technical and, where appropriate, financial assistance for technology transfer to the commodity exporting countries for the development of processing industries and for promotion of exports of value-added products.
- Rules of GATT governing the use of export taxes and export restrictions.

And requiring review and further examination before they are included in the work programme:

- Experience of the operation of the existing international commodity agreements with a view to identifying further measures that could be taken (either within the framework of the agreements or outside their framework) to address the problems posed by structural oversupply in commodities like coffee and cocoa, including action for adopting systems for supply management by producing countries.
- The adverse impact which the internal liberalisation of trade by the producing countries is having *inter alia* on prices received by farmers and on the ability of the governments to assist them in improving productivity and in ensuring the quality standards of exported commodities.
- The functioning of an international mechanism for compensating commodity exporting countries for loss of export earning, resulting from decline in commodity prices (e.g. IMF Compensatory Financing Facility and the compensatory mechanism established under the Cotonou Agreement).
- Fluctuations of prices.

- Dealing with the anti-competitive behaviour of large foreign firms.
- Improving bargaining position of producers vis-à-vis these firms.
- Adopting well-organized commodity related market information systems to enhance the transparency and improve the understanding of commodity structures.

The document ends by suggesting a procedure for taking the initiative forward through the WTO system.

The Committee on Trade and Development may, for this purpose, convene a Special Session or appoint a Subcommittee. The report of the Special Session or Subcommittee, indicating the type of action that could be taken within the framework of WTO, should be submitted to the Fifth Ministerial Conference for taking appropriate decisions.

It is further suggested that the Committee should simultaneously transmit this submission to the:

- Committee on agriculture
- Working group on trade and finance
- Working group on transfer of technology
- Working group on trade and competition policy

with the request that they should examine the aspects of the problems which fall within their mandate.

This WTO initiative differs in many respects from the initiatives taken by Oxfam and the ICO. In contrast to these other organisations, the WTO has enormous power and commands the highest degree of attention from its member countries and the world's media. Once the procedure for introducing proposals for action has been set in motion, nothing can stop them being discussed and resolved. Of course, there is every chance that many countries will oppose these suggestions and/or reject proposals for action to be taken to resolve the crisis at the many stages of negotiations that may flow from these proposals. On the other hand, the proposals offer a powerful weapon to developing countries to expose many aspects of the contradictions that arise from the double standards adopted by industrialised countries in matters relating to trade in agricultural products and to reveal the devastating effect of this aspect of economic liberalisation.

If developing countries press this issue with sufficient resolve, wealthy countries will be forced to recognise the crisis and to explain how they intend to end it.

Notes

1. C. Gresser and S. Tickell, *Mugged: Poverty in Your Coffee Cup*, Oxford: Oxfam, 17 September 2002.
2. *Guardian*, 18 September 2002.
3. *Guardian*, 7 October 2002.

CHAPTER 8

THE FACE OF OPPOSITION

In order to establish supply management programmes for tropical commodities many technical and administrative difficulties will have to be solved. In addition, supporters of these programmes will need to mount a diplomatic offensive, supported by rigorous research studies, to prove the value of their initiatives, to win support and to counter opposition to the schemes. In order to do this it will be necessary to attempt to anticipate the main arguments that are likely to be used to oppose these initiatives. Some opposition will come from organisations which genuinely wish to support tropical countries but which are wedded to less effective solutions. Some opposition will be ideologically driven. At times, it might be difficult to distinguish between the two.

Consuming countries may be divided on their attitude towards supply control. They may recognise the obvious merits of the idea, especially for the long term, but a combination of short-term interests and concern that such arrangements may be seen as weakening the neoliberal economic doctrine is likely to stimulate resistance, especially from the United States. Such resistance could manifest itself in outright and open opposition based on an economic or utilitarian argument.

Unsatisfactory as it may seem, even with attempts to address an emergency such as this one, the wheels of diplomacy turn far too slowly, and opponents of novel concepts in these circles have all the machinery they need to frustrate and delay the negotiating procedure. The obvious response to such opposition would be to build a very strong campaign aimed at promoting the supply management concept within developing countries, in development organisations and with the general public. As had been said before, many groups have recognised that commodity prices represent a key component in Third World development. Oxfam, as we have seen, has launched its own campaign to highlight the crisis and has included supply management in a raft of measures it proposes as a means of addressing the problem.

There is some danger that wider campaigns aimed at addressing the plight of farmers affected by low prices could lack focus. Many campaigning groups already fight for increased aid, the lowering of tariff barriers, better working conditions for plantation workers, ending child labour, promoting corporate responsibility, eliminating corruption, and so on. Some have a vested interest in promoting the sale of fair-trade products. This effort should continue, of course. It is necessary, however, that the diplomatic effort and awareness-raising campaign to establish supply control programmes should concentrate on this objective only.

The main opposing arguments

Disputing the evidence

Some of the arguments and evidence I have put forward in favour of supply control could be disputed. I have, for instance, made many comparisons between current commodity prices and prices paid for these goods twenty years ago. I have used this time period because the present, dominant economic ideology received its most powerful support following the election of Margaret Thatcher in Britain in 1979 and the election of Ronald Reagan in the USA in 1980. By choosing other time periods for specific commodities it might be possible to show a less obvious trend in price movements. It may also be possible, by careful selection of individual countries, to demonstrate that some developing nations have benefited from the adoption of more liberalised economic policies.

Apart from disputing existing evidence, opponents might manufacture false evidence or exaggerate the implications of some short-term trends. Tiny increases in a commodity price might be hailed as an end to the commodity crisis.

What cannot be denied, however, is the sheer scale of poverty in the Third World; nor can anyone pretend that poverty rates are falling. The UN reported in June 2002 that living standards in the world's forty-nine poorest countries, most of which depend on agricultural commodity exports, are lower now than thirty years ago. Furthermore, no amount of selected statistics can explain the hypocrisy of those countries that are forcing economic liberalisation on poor countries while maintaining strict supply control and generous subsidies for their own farmers. It has been calculated that every cow in Europe is subsidised to the tune of $2.20 a day – more than the income of almost 2 billion of the world's citizens.[1] How can anyone be convinced that agricultural trade liberalisation will serve to enrich poverty-stricken countries when those countries with the wealthiest agricultural sectors refuse to adopt such policies?

Weakening the WTO

The fundamental differences between poor and rich countries have surfaced several times in the short life of the WTO. The veneer of democratic respectability afforded by the WTO's consensus decision-making process has been marred by arguments over dollar bananas and generic drugs, and by the secret caucusing of powerful countries to manipulate negotiating agendas. On each occasion wealthy countries have countered complaints by raising the spectre of the WTO falling apart – which, they say, would leave Third World countries in an even worse position. If there were no rules-based system for international trade, so their argument goes, industrialised countries would be free to erect even higher import barriers against products from developing countries. In other words, if developing countries use the WTO to frustrate the interests of companies based in countries of the developed world, these countries will see no purpose for the WTO and will pull out of the organisation and cease to fund it, as they have with other UN bodies that they didn't find to their liking. If the WTO were to be used as the vehicle for introducing supply-control measures for tropical products, no doubt this argument would be used again. But how realistic is this threat?

Trade between industrialised countries and the world's poorest countries forms only a tiny proportion of total world trade. The importance of the WTO to wealthy countries is in its role as mediator and rule maker for trade between the world's three main trading blocs in the Far East, Europe and North America and, after that, between these blocs and the emerging economies of Southeast Asia, China and the former Eastern bloc countries. This role of the WTO is of vital importance to the programme for a narrowly defined concept of globalisation advocated by the new economic orthodoxy and it will not be abandoned to scupper the comparatively trivial issue of tropical commodity supply control.

Technical arguments

The most likely manifestation of opposition will come in the form of an exaggeration of the technical difficulties of establishing supply control systems. These problems are discussed in some detail elsewhere in this book; no one would suggest that the task of establishing these systems will be easy. Supply control is exercised in many other sectors, however, and has been successfully applied to tropical commodities in the past.

The key to solving these difficulties will be the measure of give-and-take in negotiations between the participating countries and between governments and farmers' organisations within these countries. Making a small reduction in exports by using a programme to achieve an equivalent reduction in production is a relatively simple objective provided all concerned are enthusiastically committed to the tasks they are being asked to perform and fully appraised of the likely benefits that will follow.

Reorientation of the development establishment

As we have seen, many development institutions have accumulated a vested interest in maintaining a raft of initiatives designed to help farmers but which act only to increase production and, therefore, to exacerbate the commodities crisis. Some of these institutions might even consider supply control a threat to their existence. In the end, however, development institutions have to do what their funding agencies tell them to do. Many of the projects undertaken by these agencies are useful, or at least innocuous. The fair-trade movement may be small but it does assist a number of farmers. The provision of small-scale credit facilities and the introduction of labour-saving technology can help farmers a great deal. Any technical assistance which increases food security is of vital importance. The focus of any effort to win support for supply control among these agencies would therefore be to convince them to discontinue projects which help to boost production of cash crops in favour of these more useful initiatives.

A disincentive to aid donors

Any action taken by developing countries that could increase the costs of imports for wealthy countries is likely to be met with threats to cut aid and/or the benefits of preferential trade agreements. Such threats have been made many times in the past and are likely to be faced again in this context. Each developing country will have to satisfy itself that the benefits of higher commodity prices will outweigh existing aid benefits.

Supply control, however, does offer the opportunity to shake off the shackles of aid-dependency and the benefits are likely to be high enough to risk any retaliatory action of aid donors. In addition, the increased wealth derived from higher export earnings is likely to attract more investment to establish industries to produce goods on which this increased wealth can be spent. Increased export earnings and long-term investment are a great deal more valuable and reliable than aid funds.

The trade-distorting argument

The term 'trade-distorting' has powerful connotations and is often used in the WTO as a guillotine to divide good, market-friendly measures from old-fashioned restrictive practices. It is used widely in negotiations concerning trade. The term describes government subsidies, import tariffs, preferential treatment, cartels, and so on. Some extremist *laissez-faire* economists, who believe in the unrestricted freedom of commerce, would do away with all of these trade barriers. As we have seen, however, the economic doctrine advocated by the most powerful industrialised countries falls very short of this extremist position and is very selective about which restrictions should be applied and where they should be applied.

It would be considered politically impossible for them to advocate the free movement of labour around the world, for instance. Some countries apply trade sanctions enthusiastically against those countries that they perceive to be political competitors – as the USA does with Cuba. And there are countless other duties, quotas and subsidies used to limit competition. Neoliberal economists accept this state of affairs but argue that the world should be working towards reducing these restrictions and not applying new ones. This argument is, of course, a hypocrite's charter. Nothing is done to prevent the USA from increasing its already bloated farm subsidy budget. European governments are constantly bailing out failing private-sector companies with taxpayers' money, but we hear very little complaint from these economists about such trade-distorting measures. The recent agreements to restrict aluminium and steel production so that higher prices can be restored go almost unnoticed.

The overwhelming argument in support of supply management for tropical commodities is that such measures would address the problem of grinding poverty and would thus help to save millions of lives.

The environmental argument

An environmental argument has been used to oppose supply control of certain commodities such as coffee and cocoa. If large numbers of the trees that produce these crops were cut down it would certainly damage the environment in some drier parts of the tropics. Environmentalists are also concerned that industrialisation of the Third World will increase pollution. They would also like to reduce the distance that farm products are transported between producers and consumers and are encouraging supermarkets to buy their supplies from local farmers rather than from more distant parts of the world. The environmental lobby is generally opposed to the negative effects of globalisation, and it is therefore important to address these concerns.

Clearly, any programme which included a reduction of the production of tree crops must be accompanied by appropriate measures to protect the environment, including, for instance, the planting of other types of trees. Although only a small percentage of trees may need to be destroyed, efforts must be made to make sure that they are not all cut down in one particular area or in areas with a delicately balanced ecosystem.

Encouraging the processing of primary commodities in developing countries into added-value products will certainly require the building of some factories. This will, however, replace factories currently carrying out similar activities in consuming countries and so the overall negative environmental impact would be zero. Processed products are generally less bulky than unprocessed goods. Moving them to consuming countries is likely to reduce total transport use.

What can be said with certainty, however, is that low commodity prices are a major cause of environmental degradation as farmers try to work impoverished land and hardwood trees are harvested and exported to augment diminishing foreign currency earnings.

Covert opposition

Although all the above arguments are likely to be used to oppose supply management programmes, the most powerful opposition will not surface in the public domain. It will be applied in the form of bribes, threats and blackmail and plotting behind closed doors. Enthusiastic supporters of such schemes will suddenly turn into vociferous opponents overnight without explanation. Meetings held to discuss the issue will be bogged down with technical hitches and filibustering. Key technical staff will be unexpectedly transferred during crucial periods of negotiation. Accusations of mismanagement will be made, causing delays while investigations are being carried out. Trade negotiators have become familiar with all these dirty tricks and have come to expect the unexpected.

Note

1. *New Scientist*, 21 December 2002.

CHAPTER 9

A PERSONAL ACCOUNT

Economics students are less interested in protecting the environment or helping the poor than students of other subjects. The future economist is instead mostly interested in gaining power and influence, making money and having a good time. This picture of economists as amoral and acquisitive emerges from a survey by the Open University of Israel and Tel Aviv University comparing the values and motives of 199 economics students with 165 students of other subjects. (*New Scientist*, 14 December 2002)

For those who have never observed the day-to-day life of farming communities in developing countries it is, perhaps, difficult to understand just how hard and insecure life is for a very large proportion of the people with whom we share this planet. The livelihood of these people depends on pitting their skills as farmers against the weather, plant diseases and all the other scourges of crops and animals. A farmer with possessions worth US$100 would be considered wealthy in many countries. Many plantation workers are even worse off, as they have no access to land to work for themselves and can lose their job at a moment's notice. There are very few opportunities to make a living in other occupations and access to education is very limited. Modern medical services are beyond the means of most rural people and high rates of infant mortality and serious diseases are normal – 72 per cent of the world's population has access to only 11 per cent of the world's medication. Their leaders are often weak and corrupt and social deprivation often spills over into conflict and even all-out war.

What makes this worse for these communities is that they know full well that only a few hours away by air there are countries where people spend much more on a computer game than they can afford to spend on the medicines they would need to save the life of a sick child. They also know that the cost of eradicating the levels of absolute poverty that they suffer would hardly be missed by the industrialised world. Like many people who have worked in these countries, I simply cannot understand why this massive and growing division between rich and poor is not the burning issue of our age.

The reluctance of wealthy countries to make the necessary transfer of material and intellectual resources needed to assist these people to lift themselves out of poverty is obvious. The situation, as I hope I have demonstrated, is in fact far worse. While wealthy countries sit behind lofty walls of market protection and continue to pay their farmers generous agricultural subsidies, they insist that poor countries cease to offer any support for their agricultural industries and manipulate the economies of these countries to ensure that they receive only a pittance for the only commodities they can successfully export.

We do not yet know what the full long-term consequences of this indifference might be, but presumably the governments of developed countries feel that they can control the natural consequences of this order of global inequality measured in mass migration, increases in the production of narcotics, political destabilisation and bitterness towards the industrialised world.

Of course, many people are dedicating themselves to trying to change the attitude of the governments of wealthy countries on the issue of Third World poverty. They are working on many fronts but there is a growing recognition of the double standards applied by powerful nations. The anti-globalisation movement has grown powerful enough to ensure that world leaders can only meet to manipulate the world's economic agenda in remote places guarded by thousands of armed police. The symbolism alone of this retreat has become an acute embarrassment to these political and financial bigwigs.

The leaders of several developing countries have bravely and openly expressed their contempt for the hypocrisy of powerful nations. Some churches and charities are expending huge amounts of energy to bring the plight of the poor to the attention of the public and are trying to address the extreme consequences of orthodox economic thinking, and some academics are providing theoretical analysis to support alternative ideas. Most of these efforts are very diffused, however, as, perhaps, the complexity of the cause and possible solutions for poverty may demand.

It is always difficult for people to judge the importance of an issue, if they are as close to the arguments as I am to the tropical commodity crisis. I have concluded, however, that the crisis can be overcome and, what is more, I believe that it can be used to expose the weaknesses of orthodox arguments and help developing countries to become more independent. It may even provide a useful opportunity to make the economies of these countries stronger and more sustainable.

For some years now I have attempted to make more people aware of the way I believe the commodities crisis should be addressed. I have had some success in convincing individuals that only a bold solution will match the scale of the disaster. It became apparent some years ago, however, that almost all of the institutions that have an understanding of the very serious effects of the collapse in commodity prices are prevented, for one reason or another, from thinking beyond the boundaries set for them by neoliberal economists.

There are many hundreds of agencies concerned with agricultural development in Third World countries. Some of them provide funding for research aimed at identifying ways to improve agricultural performance. The larger agencies are responsible for providing funds to smaller agencies to carry out the many thousands of practical projects designed to help farmers. Many academic institutions are involved in agricultural development and most industrialised countries have established specialised agricultural departments within their overseas development ministries. The agricultural extension services of developing countries do what they can, within very limited budgets, to assist local farmers; and, of course, many churches and non-governmental organisations fund their own agricultural development programmes.

In addition to these bodies, several of the major institutions linked to the United Nations are deeply involved in helping governments to develop improved agricultural policies and to help them carry these policies out. These include the Food and Agriculture Organisation, the UN Development Programme, the World Food Programme, the UN Conference on Trade and Development, the International Trade Centre and the International Fund for Agricultural Development. And casting its sombre shadow over all of these is the ever-present World Bank. One might have assumed that at least one of these organisations should by now have concluded that overproduction has caused the collapse of commodity prices and recommended the obvious solution of cutting output.

None of the major development agencies has carried out studies to examine the relationship between the oversupply of agricultural commodities and economic structural adjustment programmes; this is only one of several taboo development issues which are not, apparently, important enough to receive proper attention. Liberalisation appears to have the effect of stimulating some economies but not those of poor countries, which are dependent on agriculture; yet no effort is made to find out if this represents a fundamental flaw in the thinking behind neoliberal economics.

Countries like the USA and, more recently, the Asian Tigers achieved robust growth by heavily protecting their fledgling economies. We are told, however, that poor countries must dismantle any protection they have to achieve the same ends. Why is this apparent anomaly not subject to the most rigorous examination?

Dozens of official reports extol the virtues of countries like Vietnam, India and Hungary for liberalising their economies and attribute economic growth to those policies. Most of them end with rather enigmatic statements admitting that *some* developing countries, such as almost all of those in sub-Saharan Africa, for some reason not explained, have failed to respond to the universal liberalisation panacea.

Another option available to the major international donor agencies, when faced with evidence of the tropical commodities crisis, is simply to ignore it. A recent World Bank report on Burundi, where coffee accounts for 80 per cent of export earnings, failed to identify the risk of the country's enormous reliance on this single commodity, despite a whole section discussing other potential risks.[1] The IMF, similarly, failed to identify this risk in the case of Ethiopia, which is dependent on coffee exports for 63 per cent of its export earnings.[2]

For those like me who believe that very little can be done to narrow the gap between the world's rich and poor without a fundamental shift in economic thinking, this stonewalling of ideas represents a formidable obstacle. I believe that there are ways in which this institutional sclerosis can be overcome. I think it is very important, however, to understand the nature of the in-built institutional resistance to exploring solutions that contradict orthodox economic thinking. I would, therefore, like to offer an account of my experiences in trying to gain support for the idea of supply management for tropical commodities, which might throw some light on the reasons for this resistance.

I started trading in commodities almost forty years ago for a large merchant house in the City of London. In those days London was the undisputed hub of international commodity trading. The business had evolved over hundreds of years and was still an integral component of Britain's colonial history in Africa, the Caribbean and Southern Asia. Many of the larger City companies owned plantations, packing stations, warehouses, barges and transport companies. Hundreds of small, family-owned trading companies, specialising in everything from asafoetida to vetiver oil, ran their businesses from cramped offices in the Square Mile and around the docks further down the river.

My company employed agents in the former colonies to fix contracts with suppliers in arrangements that had lasted for generations. Every morning we would receive dozens of cables from our agents full of details of ships' manifests and loading dates and warning us of frosts in Brazil, storms in the Atlantic and the activities of our competitors. From all this information we were able to make judgements about the market and speculate by buying or selling the commodities in advance of delivery.

As the former colonies gained independence we had to forge new relationships with the export agencies of the new governments. They were reluctant to continue signing supply contracts on the terms we were used to and many started to employ their own sales agents in London and to sell their products directly to our customers. Many of the smaller trading companies went out of business or amalgamated with each other. There was not only less conventional business around, but the International Commodity Agreements on some of the major commodities were holding prices in a straitjacket which restricted speculative activity.

I decided to move into the metal trading business, where there was a lot more scope for the kind of risky business I seemed to be good at. Changes in technology and the expanding world economy caused the metals markets to gyrate up and down for almost twenty years, unfettered by any international agreements. These market movements encouraged wild speculation. The London Metal Exchange was affectionately dubbed 'Monte Carlo without music'.

In the world of commodity trading the bottom line becomes a tyranny of daily life. Losing money means losing your job and the means of making a profit are limited only by the international rules of trade or the fear of someone finding out that you might be breaking the law. Traders are attracted to the commodity sector because the industry is largely unregulated and because most companies offer generous bonus schemes based on the individual trader's profit. Although there are some fairly decent people in the industry, it does seem to attract exceedingly greedy individuals, especially in its higher echelons, who give little thought to the people who produce the commodities they deal in. The idea that large trading companies would voluntarily pay more for raw materials, as Oxfam proposes, is quite simply preposterous. No amount of positive publicity would induce them to cut their noses off to spite their faces.

I became interested again in the markets of agricultural commodities in 1986 when I had semi-retired from my own trading company and was starting to be employed as a consultant for the major development agencies and NGOs that needed to know more about how commodities were traded. It was really only then that I started to meet farmers and plantation workers in Third World countries and began to realise how differently they looked at commodity markets. The few cents on every kilo of produce that I had so energetically fought for to boost my profits could decide whether or not their children went to school.

One of the smaller organisations for which I acted as a consultant was Twin Trading, a not-for-profit company which bought goods from the Third World for sale in Britain. In 1989 the financial support given to the International Coffee Agreement was withdrawn by consuming countries. Twin, and several of the other organisations that engaged in what was called alternative trading, were deeply concerned that the price of tropical products would plummet as the market control systems were removed.

The Max Havelaar Foundation in the Netherlands had, for some years, been establishing principles for fair trade, especially in coffee, and various British organisations, including Twin, decided to follow in their footsteps. I was very much involved in the early stages of establishing the fair-trade coffee brand 'CaféDirect' in the UK but was never really convinced that fair trade could begin to address the growing problem of oversupply.

Once the fair-trade companies started to rely less on charitable funding and more on the income derived from sales, the work they did became an end in itself. As far as I could see, there was no pressure to examine the causes of low prices or to campaign against the effective abolition of the International Commodity Agreements. After all, if tropical commodity producers were paid a proper price for their goods under new international agreements, there would be no need for fair trade.

Mainstream advertising companies were employed by the fair-trade movement to conduct consumer surveys. They advised that advertisements should emphasise the idea that buying the products was stylish and showed good taste. The message became confused. It wasn't so easy to work out whether buying fair-trade coffee was a campaign on behalf of poor people or a fashion accessory – a pleasant and far-from-painful way of doing your bit for the poor farmers.

I developed the impression that fair trade may even be helping the governments of the major consuming countries to avoid criticism over their inaction. They could say, with some legitimacy, that those who were concerned about poverty in developing countries shouldn't blame them; they should, instead, buy fair-trade products. They found fair trade a cheap and convenient way of avoiding the problem and had nothing but praise for the idea.

The people involved in fair trade were delighted to see their products on supermarket shelves, and believed that before long a huge proportion of the population would be buying fair-trade brands. They would have found a new way of harnessing the basic decency of ordinary customers to their cause. The growth of sales was extremely slow, however. I tried to make the case for using the publicity that fair-trade products received to hammer home the message that the welfare of hundreds of millions of some of the poorest people in the world had been abandoned to a brutal and erroneous interpretation of the role that commodity markets play in the process of economic development – but no one seemed interested in the idea.

My main consultancy work over the last ten years has been with development agencies. These organisations are also intimately concerned with the deteriorating plight of tropical farmers. Over this period I have worked for or been in contact with dozens of these organisations, ranging from the largest UN agencies to small campaign groups, to press the commodity crisis issue. Many individuals working for these organisations need no convincing that the framework of international trading rules, within which they work, is negating all their efforts to help tropical farmers, but these opinions are very rarely translated into a re-examination of these rules, let alone action to change them.

There are several reasons for this blinkered approach but the core problem is funding. Agricultural development agencies spend a considerable amount of time bidding for contracts to carry out development projects. These contracts might be designed by the funding agency or they might be proposed by the individual development agency, but it is always the funding agency that decides which projects go ahead. Measuring the impact of economic liberalisation and globalisation on poor countries is a particularly sensitive topic for industrialised countries; if the terms of reference of proposals to conduct studies in this area are likely to throw up any awkward questions, such studies will not be funded.

There are some sources of independent funding – from charities and churches, for instance. The bulk of the money, however, comes from national and supranational bodies controlled ultimately by the governments of industrialised countries. Even the massive development agencies like the UN Food and Agriculture Organisation and UNCTAD will tell you that they have no money to spend on new projects unless they can persuade a wealthy member government to provide funding for them.

The funding of projects and the link between funding and the execution of development projects have undergone a significant change over the last decade or so. Most of the larger development agencies used to have a high degree of autonomy and could initiate their own projects and have them carried out by their own staff. One of the largest and most prestigious tropical agriculture research establishments was Britain's Natural Resources Institute (NRI). Its staff of 375 professionals included many world experts who were called upon to help solve problems for farmers throughout the tropics. In 1994 the British government put the NRI up for sale and the staff numbers were consequently reduced to 130. A similar fate befell the Royal Tropical Institute in Holland and many other similar institutions.

Now these agencies, almost invariably, receive only core funding to run their administrative departments, yet have to compete with rival agencies in a bidding system for the money to carry out development work. They can no longer support a permanent staff of experts, but instead hire consultants, such as myself, on short-term contracts. Many of these experts have lost their permanent jobs with the agencies and there is no shortage of people willing to carry out the work. The casualisation of this work represents a considerable saving for the agencies, but the loss of the permanent teams of specialists working together to solve problems has damaged the quality of work carried out and increased the control of funding agencies over the agenda of research.

These agencies have also tried to cut the cost of practical fieldwork. One of the strategies they use increasingly is to employ the services of non-governmental organisations to do the work on their behalf on a contractual basis. NGO staff are cheaper to employ than civil servants or permanent staff, and once the contract has been completed the funding agency ceases to take any responsibility for them. These contracts represent the main source of income for many NGOs; this ensures that they are unlikely to question the terms of reference given to them for the projects they work on. Even the largest charities that campaign on behalf of the world's poor often find it difficult to attack what has become the new orthodoxy for fear of losing their contacts with the big funding agencies.

As well as employing NGOs, there has also been a growing trend in recent years for development agencies to hire private companies, especially to carry out studies on the more commercial aspects of Third World farming. Most of these companies have more experience in agribusiness than in peasant farming. They often recommend that modern farming techniques should be introduced and that farms should be agglomerated into large, commercial entities. The cost of hiring these companies reduces the overall pool of funding available to public-sector and charitable organisations that have no direct business agenda and that have a greater understanding and concern for the social and economic impact of policy changes on rural communities in developing countries.

Some of the largest development agencies that fund development projects have become increasingly sensitive to criticism from anti-globalisation campaigners, among others. They have tried to find ways to combat this criticism mainly by spending a great deal more money on public relations, but have also realised that they need to get a better understanding of the arguments and culture of their opponents. One way of achieving this objective has been to employ many of their erstwhile critics. This not only gives them direct access to critical opinion but also serves to neuter at least a proportion of their critics. One senior manager of a fair-trade company who had spent years railing against the excesses of the World Bank was employed by them on a highly advantageous contract and now spends her time trying to get large producers in developing countries to use the New York and London futures markets.

Now that markets have been liberalised, economic analysis of the relationship between tropical farming, international trade rules and domestic economic policy should be carried out at every level in the development community. This work is now concentrated, however, only in the largest institutions. This is because smaller agricultural development agencies have not been given the necessary resources to adapt their work in the light of the changing market environment. There has been very little protest from these smaller agencies as they had no need to employ market analysts or trade economists in the past, when markets were more regulated, and so don't know what they are missing.

I have now worked on many agricultural development projects in Third World countries and met hundreds of the people who dedicate themselves to helping poor farmers. Almost all these people have a background in science. They are biologists, agronomists, entomologists, biochemists and veterinarians. They may realise that their work is entirely circumscribed by political, economic, social and market forces but they do not understand them. I was recently trying to explain my work to an energetic and well-respected agronomist who runs an agency which tries to encourage farmers to grow new types of crop for export. After some minutes he cut me short and said that he didn't want to know about Geneva. All he wanted to do was to 'get these people off their backsides and get them producing'.

People who have some understanding of how power relations express themselves through markets occupy an entirely different culture to the scientists. These fieldworkers may tolerate the odd agricultural economist or sociologist in their midst but they are deeply suspicious of any attempt to have their work guided by people with an understanding of the inexact and disquieting world of money and power. They simply want to get on with the job of breeding new varieties, increasing yields and devising ways to keep agricultural pests at bay. They are pre-programmed to increase production and many are still completely unaware that all their efforts are working against the interests of the people they are trying to help. This is not true, of course, when they are helping farmers to grow food for themselves and the local market.

The idea that farmers' difficulties can be solved with a 'technical fix' has also worsened the oversupply problem in other ways. Some of the largest agencies have encouraged farmers to grow what for them are new or non-traditional crops. Fieldworkers might have noticed, for instance, that the going price for a particular spice is high compared with the products that some particular group of farmers has traditionally grown. Great efforts are made to encourage these farmers to grow cloves or cardamoms or vanilla. No attempt is made to estimate the impact that this new production will have on the global market of these products, however, so, when the crop is harvested, the farmers discover that the market price has fallen drastically and that they are no better off than they were before. This type of mistake is made repeatedly but, as far as I can see, there has rarely been any insistence on market impact studies before the approval of such projects.

Thousands of studies are carried out each year on every conceivable aspect of tropical farming. Few are directed at the relationship between the welfare of typical small-scale farmers and the liberalisation process and almost none of these allows researchers to make any direct link with the collapse of commodity prices. The funding agencies control the terms of reference of research studies and the publication of results. They can ensure that any reports which expose the negative effects of liberalisation are buried deeply within internal records.

In order to combat the criticism of anti-globalisation campaigners, however, the giant funding agencies regularly produce statistics which are deliberately skewed to support the status quo. One common way to try to throw a positive light on the liberalisation process is to require researchers to aggregate findings on the economic impact of the new policies over a mix of developing countries that include potential economic giants like Malaysia and Thailand. These countries were highly protective while they were developing their manufacturing industries now benefit from the lowering of tariff barriers into consuming countries, but their economies bear no relation to those of, say, Malawi and Tanzania. This form of aggregation can skew statistics dramatically. For instance, an announcement was made at the Earth Summit in Johannesburg in August 2002 that 20 million fewer people went to bed hungry than was the case six years previously. In fact 70 million Chinese had been lifted out of hunger in those years but in the rest of the world 50 million *more* people went hungry.

One might have expected that, with export revenues collapsing and debts piling up, the governments of tropical countries would be, by now, the most vociferous critics of the economic policies imposed on them and the international trade rules within which they are obliged to operate. This is true only to a certain extent, and only very recently have these governments made any link between falling commodity prices and market liberalisation.

There may be several reasons for this failure on behalf of Third World governments to analyse one of their greatest economic problems. It is true that very few governments of developing countries can afford to employ people with the necessary experience and qualifications to conduct accurate research on all the many economic issues that confront them. Civil-service salaries are usually much lower than those in the private sector and development agencies in these countries and the most talented and educated professionals cannot be retained by government. This means that, for most analysis of economic issues, these governments must rely on UN and other development agencies.

Perhaps a more fundamental issue concerns the allegiance of Third World governments. One burden that most tropical farmers are spared is the payment of income tax. It could be argued that small-scale farmers bear most of the nation's tax bill because they make by far the largest contribution, through their hard labour, to the country's productivity and export revenue. They pay no taxes directly to their government, however. The largest single contributors to government revenue in most developing countries are aid and development agencies. If governments insist on policies which would help millions of people in rural communities against the advice of the agencies that fund them, they will lose aid revenue. They simply cannot fully represent the farmers' interests. Things would be different if all of these countries were fully democratic, but most are not. Many leaders cling to power for decades by manipulating the political landscape or through direct authoritarian rule. When they are replaced it is often through a military coup, which merely replaces one undemocratic group with another.

This problem calls into question the recent insistence by the World Bank, the IMF, the EU and other major aid donors that further assistance will be dependent on significant progress towards 'good governance'. When looking at these conditions in practice, the most important element generally turns out not to be increased government expenditure on education and health, the rooting out of corruption or even a greater degree of democracy. The lack of sanctions applied after the recent example of Tanzania spending US$25 million on an unnecessary, obsolete air-traffic-control system, built in Britain, shows that even aid money need not be spent on alleviating poverty if it is, instead, used to buy capital equipment from an industrialised country. Good governance principally means significant progress towards the selling off of state assets, the devolution of power to the private sector, the lowering of trade barriers and the liberalisation of agricultural markets. It would certainly not serve the interest of the industrialised countries that provide aid to encourage democracy if the process led to the population demanding democratic control over the country's assets and a refusal to comply with the international trade rules that didn't serve their interests.

Although there may be no deliberate conspiracy to control developing country governments through the aid system, this is certainly its effect. As Aminatta Forna put it recently: 'Aid and debt are the puppet masters' strings.'[3] Alfred Maizels also suggests that developed countries are deliberately failing to address the tropical commodity crisis and exploiting developing countries' desperate need for export income to exert control. 'A consideration for some developed countries', he says, 'has been that steps to alleviate this foreign exchange squeeze might well reduce leverage of the Bretton Woods institutions in the application of strict conditionality terms to their stabilisation and structural adjustment programmes.'[4]

Government corruption and government agency corruption have played a significant part in the failure of several of the many development projects that I have worked on or been closely associated with. In the years I have been working in this field and in all the hundreds of reports I have read (and in those that I have written), I have never once come across a detailed account of corruption. It is common practice in some Eastern African countries, for instance, that the police extract bribes from lorry drivers carrying agricultural produce to market. If drivers refuse to pay they will be arrested for some minor traffic offence and face a fine greater than the bribe payment. Judges and magistrates are complicit in the scam. This practice costs both the farmer and the consumer a significant amount of money. I have travelled in trucks where this has happened more than once in comparatively short journeys. When I included this account in my report I was asked to remove it as it might be seen as a criticism of the government. The same has happened when I referred to civil servants failing to turn up to meetings, or to politicians and officials employing incompetent relatives on aid programmes or spending money in an inappropriate way.

All the other researchers I have talked to have the same experience. It is simply an unwritten law that the agencies with a monopoly on government criticism are the largest national and multilateral funding agencies. Only they can choose which government misdemeanours can be referred to and which cannot. This convention gives these agencies added control over these governments.

The private sector rarely intervenes conspicuously in the formulation of government and multilateral agency policy for agriculture but has a powerful influence over the agenda within which agricultural policy is made. As I have mentioned earlier in the book, many of the largest corporations trading in tropical commodities sit on the international committees that set minimum quality standards for imports of products and supply technical advice to those committees. Executives from these companies are also seconded by governments as part of their national representation in their missions to the WTO. In many cases the policy positions of countries are hardly distinguishable from those of the large trading organisations based in these countries. The US African Growth Opportunity Act is, to all intents and purposes, run by large American corporations.

In addition, of course, large corporations have the freedom to choose where to invest, and where not to invest. The competition for this investment is very fierce, and companies ask for and receive generous tax holidays, access to services and infrastructure and many other forms of aid and exemptions from government rules and regulations. This is especially true of Free Trade Zones, where foreign companies are exempted from many controls over labour law, duties, tariffs, and so on.

Some years ago I was employed to examine a phenomenon known as transfer pricing abuse. This abuse occurs when multinational companies sell the commodities they produce in the developing countries through associate companies. They also use these associate companies to buy the capital equipment they need to operate in developing countries. They sell the commodities cheaply to the associate and buy the capital equipment expensively. In this way they artificially reduce their profits in the developing country and, by doing so, reduce their tax liability. The full profit is, of course, made outside the country, preferably in a low-tax country like Switzerland. Every company I investigated indulged in this practice to a greater or lesser extent. It has been estimated that tax avoidance is costing the developing world well over US$50 billion a year – equivalent to the total world aid budget.[5]

Developing countries must now rely more and more for their inward investment on multinational companies but, for the reasons outlined above, they may not achieve the rewards they expect from this investment.

It would be wrong to suggest that there is a small group of powerful people who can block criticism of neoliberal economics and its impact on those developing countries which are highly dependent on agriculture. All the important policy decision-making is highly concentrated, however, and the economists and trade experts who advise the diplomats and politicians who make these decisions are chosen for their unerring allegiance to orthodox, neoliberal ideology. I was talking recently to a representative of the US Agency for International Development who administered a considerable aid budget in Eastern Africa. I asked him why he was spending money on a project to help wealthy traders in the area rather than on a project to help poor farmers. He said, 'Don't keep telling me about the poor, Peter. The poor are just too damn lazy to get rich.'

The history of my attempts to shift the commodity crisis up the development issues agenda goes back to the early 1990s. I had no success in my attempts to encourage the fair-trade movement to look beyond their chosen approach. In 1995 I published a book, *Tropical Commodities and Their Markets*, which described the markets of about two hundred tropical products and showed how the market prices of all of them could only just sustain the people who produced them. I proposed that some kind of supply management would be needed to lift prices to an equitable level. I have also written articles for specialist agricultural development journals on the subject and delivered many papers on the supply management theme. At one very large conference in Paris in 2000, the audience, which included many farmers, became very angry about the situation and asked some major donor agencies what they intended to do about it. Needless to say, apart from some shoulder shrugging, no solutions were offered. I am not really surprised that, as yet, no major development agency has made it its business to investigate and intervene on this issue. What is, perhaps, more surprising is that I have never yet had a critical appraisal of the reintroduction of supply control from these agencies.

As a British citizen I decided to try to engage the British government's Department for International Development (DfID) on this issue. I know several people in the department but decided to start at the top by writing to the Minister, Clare Short, after one of her blistering public attacks on anti-globalisation protestors.

I mentioned who I was, outlined the tropical commodity crisis, and asked if the DfID might look at supply management as a possible solution. The issue was completely ignored in the reply which came from one of Ms Short's staff. I was sent pamphlets on the projects undertaken by the Department and copies of speeches made by the minister.

I persisted in my efforts, however, and was eventually rewarded with an interview with an official who has some responsibility for agricultural development issues. I am reasonably well known in my somewhat esoteric field for my work on market information systems in developing countries and for my books on related issues. For this reason, perhaps, the DfID official was extremely polite and was prepared to discuss my views on the tropical commodity crisis. He had read some of my papers on the subject but said that he was not an expert in the area and could not, therefore, offer an official reaction. Despite his admitted lack of understanding of the issues involved, however, he was quite sure that the DfID would not support any idea for market intervention.

In subsequent meetings and correspondence I was told that there was 'no point in pressing for market intervention' for a number of reasons. The USA would resist it; the history of previous interventions was not encouraging; and they couldn't see anyone 'stumping up the cash' to finance it. On this last point, they suggested that Nestlé might provide the money. They also suggested that, if I was really keen to pursue the question, I might try writing to Clare Short. They reacted like a rabbit caught in the beam of car headlights – rigid and wide-eyed. To date, they seem only interested in finding a way of turning the lights off.

I was also told that the DfID could not, itself, be responsible for developing policy. Such decisions, apparently, would have to involve the Department of Trade, the Treasury and other government departments. The nearest I got to an impression that someone in the department might eventually take the problem seriously was an acknowledgement that they 'must get a better handle on the importance of agricultural commodities to the livelihood of poor people ... and must try to devise ways to alleviate their problems'.

During this correspondence the same official who had so politely listened to my case invited me to a conference sponsored by the DfID to discuss new ways in which the DfID might assist tropical coffee and cocoa farmers. I asked if I might be allowed to make a short speech at the conference to inform the participants of my work and my ideas. This request was turned down. The conference was attended by representatives of many agricultural development agencies, the World Bank, academic institutions, major multinational trading companies and producer countries. The agenda covered all the usual approaches of fair trade, risk management, quality improvement, and so on, described earlier in this book. The multinationals' representatives felt that they were not in a strong position to help farmers directly as they nearly always dealt with them at arm's length. They did feel annoyed, however, when farmers failed to deliver goods of the right quality. Although the conference readily acknowledged that oversupply was the root cause of the farmers' problems, no proposal was made to do anything about it.

In the meantime I had been researching the impact of globalisation on the agricultural sectors of Eastern and Central African countries for a report to the International Institute for Tropical Agriculture. This is a very big subject in which the issue of commodity prices is just one component. Other issues include the dumping of subsidised agricultural goods on the region, access to market information, quality standards and the changing relationship between the Cotonou Agreement and the WTO. In the course of this research, I found it necessary to interview the representatives of these countries to the WTO in Geneva.

During these interviews I discussed, among many other things, the crisis affecting commodity prices. These representatives are diplomats and they are not expected to have any detailed knowledge of agricultural markets. They were clearly shocked to learn how far prices had fallen, and after some weeks I received an invitation to speak to a large group of representatives at a room in the WTO.

I had been to the WTO several times before but had never encountered anyone with a sense of urgency or passion about the plight of poor people. This meeting was entirely different. It was organised by the Kenyan Ambassador to the WTO and attended by the representatives who make up the Africa Group of the WTO, representatives from UNCTAD, the Commonwealth and a number of other Swiss-based development organisations. After my presentation and the discussion which followed, the representatives appeared both shocked and determined to do what they could to place the issue on the WTO agenda, in the way I have outlined in the previous chapter.

As has been said before in this book, the issue of the relationship between the way commodity markets work and poverty has all but slipped off the agenda of the main development institutions. There is no international institution designated to develop policy to ensure that producers and producing countries receive a fair reward for their products as UNCTAD once did. The WTO ambassadors are convinced, however, that the WTO is the obvious negotiating body to deal with this issue. They are in a position to use the WTO's consensus form of decision-making to make proposals for the WTO to act on this issue.

I cannot predict how the news will be received when these proposals are discussed publicly, but there are already signs that wheels are working behind the scenes to find ways to blunt this initiative. There was another meeting at the WTO on the subject, to which a wider group of interested parties were invited, including representatives from Oxfam and the Third World Network. These campaigning organisations quickly realised that the WTO ambassadors need to be backed up with as powerful a campaign as possible to expose the issue and to press for its resolution.

This meeting was also attended by Nestor Osorio, the new secretary-general of the International Coffee Organisation. He made an extremely informative and moving speech describing the plight of coffee farmers all over the world and painting a grim picture of the consequences of continuing low prices. He very much supported the ambassadors' initiative and outlined the ICO's ideas for destroying substandard stocks of coffee beans, improving the quality of coffee and promoting the product. Mr Osorio is, however, in a difficult position. The ICO cannot rely on funding from poor producing countries and has to try to accommodate the interests of the coffee trading companies and coffee consumers. He admitted that the ICO's proposals were unlikely to increase the price by very much, but I got the impression that he was reticent about openly endorsing a supply management programme.

At this time Oxfam was preparing its report on the coffee crisis, *Mugged: Poverty in Your Coffee Cup*, which served to launch their worldwide campaign on behalf of coffee farmers. They asked me for my comments on a late draft of the report and I did what I could to emphasise the pressing need to look seriously at supply management. The campaign was launched simultaneously in seventeen cities throughout world. The London venue chosen for the launch was the headquarters of the ICO in the West End of London. Latin American coffee farmers were invited to give a first-hand account of their dire circumstances, the head of Oxfam spoke, and Nestor Osorio delivered another excellent speech on the lines of the talk he had given in Geneva. The broadsheet newspapers, radio and television gave reasonable coverage to the launch of the campaign, which was accompanied in London with a stunt in which sacks of 'worthless' coffee, carried by donkeys, were dumped on the steps of the Stock Exchange.

The devastating impact of the tropical commodities crisis seems, at last, to be filtering into the agenda of the more progressive elements of the mass media and into the forums of international debate on development. As I write, there are alarming reports of another major famine in Ethiopia. Some commentators are convinced that it is poverty, not the weather, that leads to starvation in a world of surplus food. If Ethiopia earned a proper income out of coffee, its major crop, it could afford to import all the food it needs. But does it really take the death, through starvation, of tens of thousands of people to identify and address the problem of poverty?

Tropical countries will find it difficult to solve the problem for themselves. Developed countries and large corporations will not be moved to help them unless there is a groundswell of outrage from tropical farmers and the people who still have a semblance of influence over the governments of consuming countries.

Profound as the tropical commodity crisis is, it is only a symptom of a much wider issue. Developing countries have been forced into a horse race with the rest of the world in which the thoroughbreds have already churned up the turf before their heavily handicapped horse has left the starting gate. The rules of the Global Trade Handicap Race were, of course, designed by the owners of the best horses.

Modern communication systems ensure that the chief executives and major shareholders of multinational companies and government ministers of industrial countries cannot plead ignorance of the plight of billions of their fellow human beings living in poverty. They have the means to close the widening gap between rich and poor but they choose to continue advocating the system that causes it. More alarmingly, they offer the system as the only effective path to economic viability. The tropical commodity crisis is one of a growing number of phenomena – including climate change, the homogenisation of culture, gridlocked transport systems, the collapse of fish stocks, global pollution, the destruction of the rainforest and rising crime rates – that demonstrate the absurdity of this notion.

There is, of course, plenty of evidence to show that this same group of powerful people fully understand that their recipe of economic liberalisation is deeply flawed. They know that the successful economies of their own countries were not created this way. They make no effort to eliminate the tariff barriers used to protect their own industries. They continue to insist that their governments should bail out failing private-sector enterprises and fight vociferously to retain the massive government subsidies lavished on the industries of wealthy countries, including agriculture.

The cynicism of those who strive to impose their international rules governing world trade, aid and investment is driven by short-termism. Those who fashion these rules seem to find it impossible to think beyond the next dividend payment, share option or election date. Each and every proposal to assist poor countries is first scrutinised to evaluate what benefit is likely to accrue to manufacturing and service industries based in their own country.

Discussions about the cause, effect and extent of issues like pollution and global warming tend to get bogged down in the interpretation of scientific data. An examination of the tropical commodities crisis at least allows us to use the same language as those who advocate economic liberalisation as a panacea. In order to challenge those who have imposed the conditions that have led to the crisis, we need to know whether it is an unfortunate, and perhaps unforeseen, by-product of local and global economic liberalisation or whether it was considered by the proponents of liberalisation as a useful outcome of their policies. We may get closer to answering this question by examining the effect of the crisis on those who created the environment in which it occurred.

The most blatant feature of the crisis is the way it has transferred billions of dollars every year from poor farmers and poor countries to wealthy companies and countries. The liberalisation of the economies of developing countries offers another short-term bonus to wealthy countries and companies. By insisting that trade barriers, such as import tariffs, should be reduced, the markets for the goods and services within these countries can be more easily penetrated. Ironically, this feature of liberalisation also assists the wealthy world to dispose of its excess agricultural goods in developing countries.

Belief systems are so much easier to adopt when they come with a large dose of vested interest. We cannot rule out the possibility that the imposition of liberalisation has been a cynical and deliberate policy when it confers such great advantages on those who propose it.

Solving the tropical commodities crisis, massively important as that is, can only be a part of any strategy designed to address the problem of inequity. It will do very little to help the millions living in unsanitary, urban shanty towns or in countries with few or no exports; nor will it help the poor of industrialised countries. It will not reduce the massive environmental problems we face. It will not stop us measuring ourselves by what we can consume.

Finding strategies to identify the deeper causes and address the issues of poverty and environmental degradation needs to take place on a much wider front. The international forums in which these problems are discussed must represent truly the interests of those who suffer most from them. The vested short-term interests of a small minority should not be allowed to hamper these efforts. A massive change in attitude will be required to do this, and it is hard to see how such a change will come about until it is too late to do anything about these problems. But discussion of these wider issues falls well outside the scope of this book.

That said, bringing some logical order to tropical commodity markets will bring immediate relief to hundreds of millions of Third World farmers and their families. The consequences of doing nothing are just two awful to contemplate.

Notes

1. *Burundi: An Interim Strategy 1999–2001*, World Bank, Washington DC 1999.
2. *Interim Poverty Reduction Strategy Paper*, IMF and IDA Joint Staff Assessment, 2001.
3. Aminatta Forna, 'The Puppet Master's Strings', *Guardian*, 17 November 2002.
4. Alfred Maizels et al., *Commodity Supply Management by Producing Countries: A Case Study of Tropical Beverage Crops*, Clarendon Press, Oxford 1997.
5. Mark Lopiatin, *Observer*, 12 January 2003.

How Tropical Commodities Are Traded

The mechanism used for trading tropical agricultural products varies between one commodity and another, and different trading systems have evolved between different countries and different types of buyer and seller. No matter what system is used, supply management programmes should have the same effect. Nevertheless, those contemplating the introduction of systems designed to control the production and export of tropical commodities need to be familiar with the different ways these commodities are traded.

In some cases goods are sold on a long-term contractual basis. If countries wish to limit their exports from some given date under a supply management programme, such long-term deals may need to be broken or renegotiated. Governments have sovereign control over exports but may not wish to upset exporters or overseas buyers by intervening in private contractual arrangements, in which case long-term contracts may have to be allowed to run their course. Long-term contracts are rarely made at a fixed price, however. Prices for goods in these contracts are usually based on some formula fixing the price to some changing benchmark price published by a trade journal or commodity futures market. Such benchmark prices move up and down to reflect changing market conditions. This means that, in nearly all cases, the contractual price for the goods sold within a long-term contractual arrangement will rise, according to the price formula, as export or production-control mechanisms begin to reduce supplies.

Most tropical commodities produced for the export market are traded informally. That is to say, they are not traded in public auction or on some terminal or futures market. The deals are between sellers and buyers and they alone have access to the details of the contract – price, delivery date, quantity, quality, terms of payment, and so on. In some cases an agent employed either by the buyer or seller acts as an intermediary. In developing countries the major international traders often employ local agents to scour the local markets for the produce they want to buy or to set up longer-term supply contracts with producers or local merchants. These sales or purchasing agents are usually paid on a commission basis.

Once the contract of sale has been agreed, arrangements have to be made with banks or other financial institutions to open letters of credit or otherwise establish payment terms. Deals then have to be made with transport companies and shipping lines to move the goods, and, in the case of perishable items, temperature-controlled containers have to be delivered to the point of loading. Customs declarations have then to be drawn up and submitted together with insurance certificates, certificates of origin, weight and quality certificates and, in the case of food products, phyto-sanitary certificates. Once the goods have begun their journey to their destination, the supplier needs to invoice the buyer and deliver any other agreed paperwork, including bills of lading or air waybills.

The completion of all these arrangements is clearly beyond the skills and capacity of typical tropical farmers. Before economic liberalisation much of this trade was conducted by marketing boards controlled by the government of the exporting country. Now that most of these boards have been dismantled, all these arrangements have to be made by large local or transnational trading companies. This has increased the bargaining power of these companies over the individual producers.

Another trading facility available to large traders and not to small-scale farmers is the ability to hedge their transaction on one or other of the world's many futures markets. Hedging is really a method of ensuring a fixed selling or purchase price for goods delivered at some point in the future. This facility is especially important in markets that move up and down in a volatile and unpredictable pattern over short periods of time.

Several commodities grown in the tropics are traded on futures markets. These are sugar, coffee, cocoa and palm oil, cotton, maize, potatoes, sorghum, castor oil, jute and rice. Futures markets can be understood as a link between financial institutions and the commodity trade. Their origins date back to the nineteenth century, when merchants needed to finance their commodity trading with money from banks and investment funds.

The futures market can be used to help some of the larger actors in the markets to obtain credit and to reduce risks associated with unpredictable, short-term fluctuations in the market price. For this reason UNCTAD and the World Bank have established programmes to assist larger actors in the agricultural sectors of developing countries to learn about futures markets and to use them if it is appropriate for them to do so. Futures markets also give a reference price to a commodity at any given time.

In a futures market the seller promises to sell a certain quantity of a certain commodity at an agreed price, delivered to a specific location, to the buyer at a specific date in the future. The buyer might be a consumer of the commodity who wishes to cover their needs for that future date. On the other hand, the buyer might be a bank, a financial institution or a private individual who wants to make a speculative purchase because they believe that the price of the commodity will rise before the date agreed for delivery. They hope to sell the commodity at a profit before they are required to take delivery of it.

The seller may also be a banker or investor. They would have taken the view that the price will fall before the agreed delivery date. They will have promised to deliver the goods even though they do not yet own them. If they are right, and the price does fall, they can buy the goods through the futures market nearer the delivery date at less than the price they have promised to sell them at and make a profit.

Most of the buyers and sellers on the futures markets never actually see the commodities in which they trade. For them, the market is just a means of making money. Consumers and producers are able to use these markets to their advantage, however. One useful aspect of a futures market for consumers and producers is its facility to provide a means of hedging a purchase or a sale. But what does the word 'hedging' mean and why can it be useful?

Hedging

Many commodities markets are very volatile – prices go up and come down unpredictably. This makes life difficult for consumers. Let us take the example of a chocolate producer who needs to make a sales contract with a supermarket chain to sell millions of chocolate bars at a fixed price for the whole of the following year. Nobody knows what the price of cocoa is going to be at the time the chocolate-maker needs to buy the cocoa to produce the chocolate. On the futures market, however, the chocolate-maker can find a seller who is willing to supply cocoa at a fixed price for the delivery date he needs. If the price goes up on the world market, the buyer still gets his cocoa at the price agreed with the futures market seller. This type of transaction is known as hedging.

In practice the cocoa buyer, in this example, will only make paper transactions on the futures markets. Although futures markets theoretically allow for delivery of real commodities from the seller to the buyer, it is not their principal purpose and it rarely happens. In this example, the cocoa buyer will sell back the cocoa to the futures market at about the same time he needs physical delivery of the cocoa, and make a profit (since the price has gone up since he bought it). He will simultaneously purchase the same amount of real bags of cocoa, say from Ghana, and, although the price he will pay for this cocoa will be higher than the price he paid for his original purchase on the futures market (again because the price has gone up in the meantime), the difference will be covered by the profit he makes on the futures transactions.

If the price falls, rather than rises, in this period, the cocoa buyer will make a loss on his transaction on the futures market but be able to buy the physical cocoa from Ghana at the lower, prevailing price. So whether the world market price goes up or down, the buyer has managed to buy his forward requirements of cocoa at a fixed price, which enables him to sell his chocolate bars to the supermarket chain at a fixed price.

Producers of commodities also use futures markets for hedging. They can make forward sales at fixed prices and use the sales contracts as collateral to borrow money from the banks to finance their production costs. They may also wish to hedge if they feel that the price of the commodity they produce will fall before they can deliver it to a customer.

Buyers are not required to pay the total value of a purchase they make on the futures markets at the time the purchase is made. The buyer is required, however, to pay what is called a margin. This may only be a few per cent of the value of the purchase – the exact sum payable depends on the particular commodity and futures market used. If a buyer has bought a commodity on the market and its price falls between the time of purchase and the agreed delivery date, however, he will be asked for a 'margin call'. This means that the buyer has to pay an extra sum of money, which would equal the loss he would make if he sold his purchase at the prevailing market price. If the price continues to fall, he will be asked to continue covering this potential loss with more margin calls. All these sums of money, plus any interest they earn, will be taken into account when the transaction is finalised.

Options

Other devices for hedging on futures markets are available to commodity producers and consumers. These are known as options – a form of transaction called 'derivatives' on futures markets. To describe the function of an option, let us take the case of a large coffee producer or trader who wants to fix the price of a future shipment of coffee beans. He can purchase what is called a 'put-option' on the futures market covering a sale of the quantity of coffee he expects to have for sale, say, in six months' time. Buying the put-option is really buying the right to sell at a fixed price for that date but still retaining the right not to sell if the price in the intervening time increases above that fixed price. The cost of the option is known as the 'premium' and the cost of the premium varies according to the option seller's perception of the risk involved. This perception is often based on the previous record of price volatility of the commodity concerned but is usually a few per cent of the price.

The advantage of buying put-options as a means of hedging for sellers is that they can insure against a large fall in the future price of the commodity. At the same time, however, they can retain the option of cancelling the option (thus losing the premium) and selling at a higher price if the price of the commodity significantly increases. The disadvantages are that premiums can be expensive and that the market must be continuously scrutinised in order to decide whether to retain the option or cancel it. It should also be said that using these devices often encourages unwise speculation.

Using futures markets

Buyers and sellers are not able to trade directly in the futures markets. They have to use the services of brokers, who are specialist dealers and members of the market in question. Only they are allowed to transact business in that market, but they act on behalf of many clients, buying and selling on the futures market according to their clients' instructions. In most futures markets brokers are also allowed to deal on their own account. This has led to a conflict of interest on some occasions, and clients should be wary of taking their broker's advice regarding whether they think the market is going up or down, unless they know and trust the broker very well.

Buyers and sellers who wish to use futures markets must pay their brokers a commission fee on each transaction they make. This fee varies according to which market is used, what commodity is traded and the size of the transaction, but it is usually a fraction of 1 per cent of the value of the transaction. The broker, who is also responsible for setting and collecting margins and margin calls, is only likely to do business on behalf of clients that he knows are able to meet any financial commitment they make. For this reason they only accept clients with good financial references.

Futures markets do not allow trades of less than a certain minimum quantity or 'lot' of any given commodity. The value of one lot usually exceeds US$10,000, so only those interested in hedging or investing on a large scale can make use of the market.

The volume of trade in a commodity has to be very large indeed for it to be worth setting up a futures market to trade in it. Furthermore, only commodities whose qualities can be objectively and simply defined are traded on futures markers. (Billions of dollars' worth of diamonds and oil paintings are bought and sold each year but they are not traded on futures markets. Their quality is based on subjective opinion and cannot be defined simply enough for forward purchase or sale.)

Different futures markets specialise in different commodities. This sometimes depends on their location. The Chicago market dominates futures trade in soya because it is located near the world's largest soya-growing area; silk futures are traded in Japan; Malaysia has a huge rubber trading market, and so on. Some futures markets dominate trade in a particular commodity for historical reasons. The Paris market specialises in white sugar, for instance, and the New York market is looked on the world over as the market marker in arabica coffee.

There are about twenty internationally recognised futures markets, based mainly in the major financial centres of the world. Some have a very small turnover and are used almost exclusively by local traders and investors and only trade in one or two locally produced commodities.

Only large-scale traders, producers and consumers of tropical products are likely to be financially strong enough to be able to make use of a futures market. It is important for all those who are involved with these commodities to take notice of the prices trading on these exchanges, however. The volume of transactions on these futures markets is very large, often larger than the entire global turnover of the physical commodity in question, because most of the volumes of trade on the markets are paper transactions. For this reason the prices traded for the commodities on futures markets carry great authority. The prices reflect the net results of transactions carried out by the experts employed by all the bankers, investors, traders, producers and consumers who use the market. If most of the transactions in a commodity required to be delivered six months hence take place at a lower price on one day than they did on the previous day, it is likely to mean that deliveries for that future date are going to be more plentiful than was previously estimated. Price trends show the changing balance between world supply and demand.

Since so many people respect the ability of the futures markets to reflect the true market price of commodities, the markets are also used by buyers and sellers who wish to use a price formula in the contracts they make. Let us suppose that a large Kenyan coffee producer needs to make a sale of 100 tonnes of his arabica coffee, which he expects to be able to deliver to a port in November. Rather than agree to sell to the dealer at a fixed price, he may agree to use something like the following price clause in his sales contract: 'The sales price on a CIF London basis will be fixed at 5 US cents per pound discount to the closing prompt-month New York coffee market 'c' contract price as traded on the first day of November.' This so-called pricing facility offered by the futures markets is probably most useful to all those involved in the commodity concerned, whether or not they actually use the market to make transactions.

Complicated and variable as all these trading arrangements may sound, they do not represent any impediment to supply management programmes. They are merely methods of facilitating trade, not mechanisms to influence the market price. That is not to say that these systems cannot be used to manipulate markets. Speculators influenced markets for thousands of years before futures markets were invented. The introduction of supply management will tend, however, drastically to reduce speculation as supply managers control the volatility of the market.

THE USES OF TROPICAL COMMODITIES IN THE MODERN WORLD

Hundreds of different commodities are produced in the tropical regions of the world. Although synthetic substitutes have replaced some products, others have found new uses in modern medicine, industry and food processing. Ethnic minorities living in industrialised countries represent the main export market for some tropical goods, but the consumption of tropical fruit and spices has increased throughout the world as consumers explore new cuisines.

This list of the uses of tropical commodities is by no means complete but it should convey some idea of how indispensable tropical commodities are in the modern world.

Abaca	high quality ropes
Allspice	spice
Aloe vera	drugs and cosmetics
Annatto seed	cheese colouring
Arrowroot	soup and sauce thickener
Asafoetida	spice
Avocado	fruit and ingredient in cosmetics
Balsam	perfume fixative and medicine
Bamboo	furniture and construction
Banana	fruit
Betel nut	stimulant
Brazil nut	food
Camphor	plasticiser for cellulose nitrate and in medicine
Cananga oil	perfume

Candelilla wax	furniture polish
Carnauba wax	furniture and car polish
Cashew nut	food
Cassava	food and cattle fodder
Cassia	spice
Castor seed	hydrolic fluid, drying agent, medicine, adhesive, insecticides, wetting and drying agent, greases, fungicides, jet engine lubricant and fabric softener
Chillies	flavouring and food
Cinnamon	spice
Citronella oil	perfume for soap, household cleaners, etc.
Cloves	spice and *kretek* cigarettes
Cochineal	food colouring
Cocoa	chocolate and beverages
Coconut	confectionery, food, vegetable oil, doormats (fibre), and activated carbon filters (shell)
Coffee	beverage and flavouring
Cola nut	cola drinks and stimulant
Copal gum	varnish
Coriander	spice
Cotton	cloth
Cowpea	cattle fodder
Cumin	spice
Curare	muscle relaxant and anaesthetic for eye operations
Custard apple	fruit
Cutch	silk dying and tanning agent
Dates	fruit
Derris	'organic' insecticide
Durian	fruit
Eucalyptus oil	medicines and perfume
Fenugreek	spice
Frankincense	perfume
Galangal	spice
Ghatti gum	oil drilling mud
Ginger	spice
Groundnut	food and oil
Guar gum	oil drilling mud, flocculant, in explosives, textile industry, cosmetics, printers' ink, thickening agent in sauces, ice cream, etc.

Guarana	stimulant, 'buzz' chewing gum
Guava	fruit
Gum Arabic	confectionery, in brewing and printing
Hemp	ropes and sacks
Henna	dye
Indigo	dye
Ipecacuanha	purgative and emetic
Jojoba	cosmetics
Jute	ropes, carpets and sacks
Kapoc	stuffing in upholstery
Karaya gum	colostomy bags, dental fixative, dye and ink thickener
Kava	stimulant
Kumquat	fruit
Lemongrass	flavouring, detergent perfume
Lime	fruit
Locust bean gum	soup and baby-food thickener
Logwood	dye
Logan	fruit
Loofah	bath scrub
Lychee	fruit
Macadamia nut	food
Mace	spice
Maize	food
Mango	fruit
Mangosteen	fruit
Molasses	rum and cattle food
Myrrh	perfume
Neem	pesticide, in soap, toothpaste and medicines
Nutmeg	spice
Nux vomica	respiratory stimulant
Okra	food
Ouricuri wax	furniture polish
Palm oil	vegetable oil, soap, lubricants, skin creams, *napalm*
Palm kernel oil	soap, artificial cream
Pan	stimulant
Papaya	fruit and meat tenderiser
Passion fruit	fruit
Patchouli oil	perfume

Pecan nuts	food
Pepper	spice
Physalis	fruit
Physic nut	purgative
Piassava	heavy duty brooms
Pineapple	fruit
Plantain	food
Quassia amara	treatment for roundworm and fevers
Quallaia	to produce 'head' on root beer and ginger beer, shampoos, foam baths
Quinine	malaria treatment and in tonic water
Quinoa	food
Rambutan	fruit
Ramie	fibre for upholstery
Rattan	furniture
Rice	food, alcoholic wine and starch
Rubber	tyres, gloves, rubber bands, hoses, carpet backing, footwear, condoms, seals, toys, conveyor belts, adhesives, handle grips, erasers
Safflower seed	salad oil, baby food
Saffron	colouring and spice
Sago	food, sauce thickener
Sandalwood oil	perfume, fans
Sarsaparilla	flavouring
Senna	laxative
Sesame seed	cooking oil and on hamburger buns, etc.
Shea butter	cooking oil and cosmetics
Shellac	French polish, perfume industry
Silk	cloth fibre
Sisal	ropes, agricultural binding twine and sacks
Sorghum	food, cattle cake
Star anise	spice and flavouring for absinthe
Star fruit	fruit
Strophanthus	vascular stimulant
Sugar	flavouring, alcohol, fuel
Sweet potato	food, starch
Tamarind	flavouring in food and drink
Taro	food
Tea	beverage

Tobacco	stimulant
Tragacanth gum	food thickener and food stabiliser
Tung oil	varnishes
Turmeric	spice and food colouring
Vanilla	flavouring
Vetiver oil	soap and deodorants
Yam	food, birth control pills, steroids
Ylang-ylang oil	perfume

BIBLIOGRAPHY

Publications

Akiyama, T. and Larson, D. 1994. *The Adding-Up Problem*, Washington DC: World Bank.

Badiane, O. and Mukherjee, N. 1998. *Global Market Developments and African Exporters of Agricultural Commodities*, Washington DC: World Bank/International Food Policy Research Institute.

Berthelot, P., 2002. *Commodity Trade: The Path to Unsustainable Development*, London: Commonwealth Secretariat.

Caufield, C., 1997. *Masters of Illusion: The World Bank and the Poverty of Nations*, London: Macmillan.

Chang, Ha-Joon, 2002. 'Development Strategy in Historical Perspective', London: Anthem Press.

Commonwealth Secretariat, 2001. *A Study of the Assistance and Representation Needs of Developing Countries without WTO Permanent Representation in Geneva*, London: Commonwealth Secretariat.

Corea, G., 1992. *Taming Commodity Markets*, Manchester: Manchester University Press,

Digges, P., Gordon, A. and Marter, A., 1997. *International Markets for African Exports: Agricultural Reform and Agricultural Exports*, Chatham: Natural Resources Institute.

Engberg-Pedersen, P., Gibbon, P., Raikes, P. and Udsholt, L., 1996. *Limits of Adjustment in Africa*, Oxford: James Currey.

FAO, 2001. *Production Year Book*, Rome: FAO.

Finn, J., 1998. *Decision-making in the World Trade Organisation: Continuing the Reforms in Agricultural Trade*, Geneva: WTO Secretariat.

Fowler, P., 1996. *The Marrakesh Decision, Honouring the Commitment to Net-Food-Importing Countries*, London: Catholic Institute for International Relations.

Friis-Hansen, E., 2000. *Agricultural Policy in Africa after Adjustment*, Copenhagen: Centre for Development Research.

Gresser, C. and Tickell, S., 2002. *Mugged: Poverty in Your Coffee Cup*, Oxford: Oxfam.

Hanlon, J., 2001. *Mozambique and the Potential for a Campaign in Europe on Sugar*, Oxford: Oxfam.

HTS Development, 2001. *Rural Development; A Review of International Agency Approaches*, Hemel Hempstead: HTS Development Ltd.

HTS Development, 2001. *Understanding Beverage Production in Africa and Adopting Appropriate Policies for Poverty Reduction*, Hemel Hempstead: HTS Development Ltd.

IMF and IDA Joint Staff Assessment, 2001. *Interim Poverty Reduction Strategy Paper*. Washington, DC: International Monetary Fund.

Konandreas, P., 2000. *Overview of Implementation Experiences and Possible Negotiating Objectives*, Rome: FAO.

Konandreas, P., Sharma, R. and Greenfield, J., 1999. *The Agreement on Agriculture: Some Preliminary Assessment from the Experience So Far*, Rome: FAO Commodities and Trade Division.

Kwa, A. and Bello, W., 1998. *Guide to the Agreement on Agriculture: Technicalities and Trade Tricks Explained*, Bangkok: Focus on the Global South, Chulalongkorn University.

Lall. D., *Limits of Adjustment in Africa*, 1994. Oxford: James Currey.

Madeley, J., 1996. *Trade and the Hungry: How International Trade is Causing Hunger*, Geneva: World Council of Churches.

Madeley, John, 2000. *Hungry for Trade*, London: Zed Books.

Maizels, Sir Alfred, et al., 1997. *Commodity Supply Management by Producing Countries: A Case Study of the Tropical Beverage Crops*, Oxford: Clarendon Press.

Murphy, Sophia, 1999. *Trade and Food Security: An Assessment of the Uruguay Round Agreement on Agriculture*, London: Institute for Agriculture and Trade Policy, CIIR.

Prosi Magazine, 2001. 'Possible Impacts of EBA on the Agricultural Sector', *Prosi Magazine*, Mauritius.

Raffaelli, M., 1995. *Rise and Demise of Commodity Agreements*, Cambridge: Woodhead.

Robbins, P., 2000. *Review of Market Information Systems*, Kampala: Technical Centre for Agriculture (CTA).

Robbins, P., 1995. *Tropical Commodities and Their Markets*, London: Kogan Page.

Robbins, P. and Ferris, S., 2002. *The Impact of Globalisation on the Agricultural Sectors of Eastern and Central African Countries*, Kampala: International Institute of Tropical Agriculture.

Shepherd, A., 1997. *Market Information Services: Theory and Practice*, Rome: FAO.

South Centre, 1998. *The WTO Multilateral Trade Agenda and the South*, Geneva: South Centre.

UN General Assembly, 2000. *World Commodity Trends and Prospects*, New York: United Nations.

UNCTAD, *World Commodity Survey 2000–2001*, Geneva: UNCTAD.

UNCTAD/Common Fund for Commodities, 2001. *The Role of Commodities in LDCs*, Geneva: UNCTAD.

World Bank, 1994. *Adjustment in Africa*, Washington DC: World Bank.

World Bank, 2001. *Globalization can Work for Africa*, Washington DC: World Bank.

World Bank, 1999. *Burundi: An Interim Strategy 1999–2001*, Washington DC: World Bank.

Websites

Economist: www.economist.com

European Centre for Development Policy Management: www.oneworld.org

European Commission: www.europa.eu.int

Federal Reserve Bank of Minneapolis: www.minneapolisfed.org

Food and Agricultural Organisation: fao.org

International Coffee Organisation: www.ico.org

International Institute for Trade and Sustainable Development: www.ictsd

Public Ledger: www.public-ledger.com

South Centre: southcentre.org

Third World Network: www.twnside.org

World Bank: worldbank.org

World Trade Organisation: www.wto.org

INDEX

About this Series

'Communities in the South are facing great difficulties in coping with global trends. I hope this brave new series will throw much needed light on the issues ahead and help us choose the right options.'

MARTIN KHOR, *Director,*
Third World Network, Penang

'There is no more important campaign than our struggle to bring the global economy under democratic control. But the issues are fearsomely complex. This Global Issues series is a valuable resource for the committed campaigner and the educated citizen.'

BARRY COATES, *Director,*
World Development Movement (WDM)

'Zed Books has long provided an inspiring list about the issues that touch and change people's lives. The Global Issues series is another dimension of Zed's fine record, allowing access to a range of subjects and authors that, to my knowledge, very few publishers have tried. I strongly recommend these new, powerful titles and this exciting series.'

JOHN PILGER, *author*

'We are all part of a generation that actually has the means to eliminate extreme poverty world-wide. Our task is to harness the forces of globalization for the benefit of working people, their families and their communities – that is our collective duty. The Global Issues series makes a powerful contribution to the global campaign for justice, sustainable and equitable development, and peaceful progress.'

GLENYS KINNOCK, MEP

THE GLOBAL ISSUES SERIES

Already available

Walden Bello, *Deglobalization: Ideas for a New World Economy*

Robert Ali Brac de la Perrière and Franck Seuret, *Brave New Seeds: The Threat of GM Crops to Farmers*

Oswaldo de Rivero, *The Myth of Development: The Non-viable Economies of the 21st Century*

Joyeeta Gupta, *Our Simmering Planet: What to do about Global Warming?*

Nicholas Guyatt, *Another American Century? The United States and the World after 2000*

Martin Khor, *Rethinking Globalization: Critical Issues and Policy Choices*

John Madeley, *Food for All: The Need for a New Agriculture*

John Madeley, *Hungry for Trade: How the Poor Pay for Free Trade*

A.G. Noorani, *Islam and Jihad: Prejudice versus Reality*

Riccardo Petrella, *The Water Manifesto: Arguments for a World Water Contract*

Peter Robbins, *Stolen Fruit: The Tropical Commodities Disaster*

Vandana Shiva, *Protect or Plunder? Understanding Intellectual Property Rights*

Harry Shutt, *A New Democracy: Alternatives to a Bankrupt World Order*

David Sogge, *Give and Take: What's the Matter with Foreign Aid?*

Paul Todd and Jonathan Bloch, *Global Intelligence: The World's Secret Services Today*

In preparation

Peggy Antrobus, *The International Women's Movement: Issues and Strategies*

Amit Bhaduri and Deepak Nayyar, *Free Market Economics: The Intelligent Person's Guide to Liberalization*

Greg Buckman, *Globalization: Shrink or Sink?*

Julian Burger, *First Peoples: What Future?*

Graham Dunkley, *Free Trade: Myth, Reality and Alternatives*

Ha-Joon Chang and Ilene Grabel, *Reclaiming Development: What Works, What Doesn't – An Economic Policy Handbook*

Susan Hawley and Morris Szeftel, *Corruption: Privatization, Transnational Corporations and the Export of Bribery*

Damien Millet and Eric Toussaint, *Who Owns Who? Fifty Questions about World Debt*

Roger Moody, *Digging the Dirt: The Modern World of Global Mining*

Kavaljit Singh, *The Myth of Globalization: Ten Questions Everyone Asks*

Nedd Willard, *The Drugs War: Is This the Solution?*

For full details of this list and Zed's other subject and general catalogues, please write to: The Marketing Department, Zed Books, 7 Cynthia Street, London NI 9JF, UK or email Sales@zedbooks. demon.co.uk
Visit our website at: www.zedbooks.demon.co.uk

Participating Organizations

Both ENDS A service and advocacy organization which collaborates with environment and indigenous organizations, both in the South and in the North, with the aim of helping to create and sustain a vigilant and effective environmental movement.

> Damrak 28-30, 1012 LJ Amsterdam, The Netherlands
> Phone: +31 20 623 0823   Fax: +31 20 620 8049
> Email: info@bothends.org
> Website: www.bothends.org

Catholic Institute for International Relations (CIIR) CIIR aims to contribute to the eradication of poverty through a programme that combines advocacy at national and international level with community-based development.

> Unit 3, Canonbury Yard, 190a New North Road, London N1 7BJ, UK
> Phone +44 (0)20 7354 0883   Fax +44 (0)20 7359 0017
> Email: ciir@ciir.org
> Website: www.ciir.org

Corner House The Corner House is a UK-based research and solidarity group working on social and environmental justice issues in North and South.

> PO Box 3137, Station Road, Sturminster Newton, Dorset DT10 1YJ, UK
> Tel.: +44 (0)1258 473795   Fax: +44 (0)1258 473748
> Email: cornerhouse@gn.apc.org
> Website: www.cornerhouse.icaap.org

Council on International and Public Affairs (CIPA) CIPA is a human rights research, education and advocacy group, with a particular focus on economic and social rights in the USA and elsewhere around the world. Emphasis in recent years has been given to resistance to corporate domination.

> 777 United Nations Plaza, Suite 3C, New York, NY 10017, USA
> Tel. +1 212 972 9877   Fax +1 212 972 9878
> E-mail: cipany@igc.org
> Website: www.cipa-apex.org

Dag Hammarskjöld Foundation The Dag Hammarskjöld Foundation, established 1962, organises seminars and workshops on social, economic and cultural issues facing developing countries with a particular focus on alternative and innovative solutions. Results are published in its journal *Develpment Dialogue*.

Övre Slottsgatan 2, 753 10 Uppsala, Sweden.
Tel.: +46 18 102772   Fax: +46 18 122072
e-mail: secretariat@dhf.uu.se
Website: www.dhf.uu.se

Development GAP   The Development Group for Alternative Policies
is a Non-Profit Development Resource Organization working with
popular organizations in the South and their Northern partners in support of a development that is truly sustainable and that advances social
justice.

927 15th Street NW, 4th Floor, Washington, DC, 20005, USA
Tel.: +1 202 898 1566   Fax: +1 202 898 1612
E-mail: dgap@igc.org
Website: www.developmentgap.org

Focus on the Global South   Focus is dedicated to regional and
global policy analysis and advocacy work. It works to strengthen the
capacity of organizations of the poor and marginalized people of the
South and to better analyse and understand the impacts of the globalization process on their daily lives.

C/o CUSRI, Chulalongkorn University, Bangkok 10330, Thailand
Tel.: +66 2 218 7363 Fax: +66 2 255 9976
Email: Admin@focusweb.org
Website: www.focusweb.org

Inter Pares   Inter Pares, a Canadian social justice organization, has
been active since 1975 in building relationships with Third World
development groups and providing support for community-based
development programs. Inter Pares is also involved in education and
advocacy in Canada, promoting understanding about the causes, effects
and solutions to poverty.

58 rue Arthur Street, Ottawa, Ontario, KIR 7B9 Canada
Phone +1 613 563 4801   Fax +1 613 594 4704

Public Interest Research Centre   PIRC is a research and campaigning group based in Delhi which seeks to serve the information needs of
activists and organizations working on macro-economic issues concerning finance, trade and development.

142 Maitri Apartments, Plot No. 28, Patparganj, Delhi 110092, India
Phone: +91 11 2221081/2432054   Fax: +91 11 2224233
Email: kaval@nde.vsnl.net.in

Third World Network   TWN is an international network of groups and individuals involved in efforts to bring about a greater articulation of the needs and rights of peoples in the Third World; a fair distribution of the world's resources; and forms of development which are ecologically sustainable and fulfil human needs. Its international secretariat is based in Penang, Malaysia.

228 Macalister Road, 10400 Penang, Malaysia
Tel.: +60 4 226 6159   Fax: +60 4 226 4505
Email: twnet@po.jaring.my
Website: www.twnside.org.sg

Third World Network–Africa   TWN–Africa is engaged in research and advocacy on economic, environmental and gender issues. In relation to its current particular interest in globalization and Africa, its work focuses on trade and investment, the extractive sectors and gender and economic reform.

2 Ollenu Street, East Legon, PO Box AN19452, Accra-North, Ghana.
Tel.: +233 21 511189/503669/500419   Fax: +233 21 511188
email: twnafrica@ghana.com

World Development Movement (WDM)   The World Development Movement campaigns to tackle the causes of poverty and injustice. It is a democratic membership movement that works with partners in the South to cancel unpayable debt and break the ties of IMF conditionality, for fairer trade and investment rules, and for strong international rules on multinationals.

25 Beehive Place, London SW9 7QR, UK
Tel.: +44 (0)20 7737 6215   Fax: +44 (0)20 7274 8232
E-mail: wdm@wdm.org.uk
Website: www.wdm.org.uk

The Technical Centre for Agricultural and Rural Cooperation (CTA) was established in 1983 under the Lomé Convention between the ACP (African, Caribbean and Pacific) Group of States and the European Union Member States. Since 2000, it has operated within the framework of the ACP–EC Cotonou Agreement.

CTA's tasks are to develop and provide services that improve access to information for agricultural and rural development, and to strengthen the capacity of ACP countries to produce, acquire, exchange and utilize information in this area. CTA's programmes are designed to: provide a wide range of information products and services and enhance awareness of relevant information sources; promote the integrated use of appropriate communication channels and intensify contacts and information exchange (particularly intra-ACP); and develop ACP capacity to generate and manage agricultural information and to formulate ICM strategies, including those relevant to science and technology. CTA's work incorporates new developments in methodologies and cross-cutting issues such as gender and social capital.

CTA, Postbus 380, 6700 AJ Wageningen, The Netherlands.

THIS BOOK IS ALSO AVAILABLE
IN THE FOLLOWING COUNTRIES

CARIBBEAN

Ian Randle Publishers
11 Cunningham Avenue
Box 686, Kingston 6,
Jamaica, W.I.
Tel: 876 978 0745/0739
Fax: 876 978 1158
email: ianr@colis.com

EGYPT

MERIC
(Middle East Readers'
Information Center)
2 Bahgat Ali Street,
Tower D/Apt. 24
Zamalek, Cairo
Tel: 20 2 735 3818/3824
Fax: 20 2 736 9355

FIJI

University Book Centre,
University of South
Pacific,
Suva
Tel: 679 313 900
Fax: 679 303 265

GHANA

EPP Book Services,
PO Box TF 490,
Trade Fair,
Accra
Tel: 233 21 778347
Fax: 233 21 779099

MAURITIUS

Editions Le Printemps
4 Club Road
Vacoas
Tel: 696 1017

MOZAMBIQUE

Sul Sensações
PO Box 2242,
Maputo
Tel: 258 1 421974
Fax: 258 1 423414

NAMIBIA

Book Den
PO Box 3469
Shop 4,
Frans Indongo Gardens
Windhoek
Tel: 264 61 239976
Fax: 264 61 234248

NEPAL

Everest Media Services,
GPO Box 5443, Dillibazar
Putalisadak Chowk
Kathmandu
Tel: 977 1 416026
Fax: 977 1 250176

NIGERIA

Mosuro Publishers
52 Magazine Road
Jericho, Ibadan
Tel: 234 2 241 3375
Fax: 234 2 241 3374

PAKISTAN

Vanguard Books
45 The Mall
Lahore
Tel: 92 42 735 5079
Fax: 92 42 735 5197

PAPUA NEW GUINEA

Unisearch PNG Pty Ltd
Box 320, University
National Capital District
Tel: 675 326 0130
Fax: 675 326 0127

PHILIPPINES

IBON Foundation, Inc.
3rd Floor SCC Bldg,
4427 Int. Old Sta. Mesa,
Manila, Philippines 1008
Tel: 632 713 2729/2737
Fax: 632 716 0108

RWANDA

Librairie Ikirezi
PO Box 443
Kigali
Tel/Fax: 250 71314

TANZANIA

TEMA Publishing Co Ltd
PO Box 63115
Dar Es Salaam
Tel: 255 22 2113608
Fax: 255 22 2110472

UGANDA

Aristoc Booklex Ltd
PO Box 5130,
Kampala Road
Diamond Trust Building
Kampala
Tel: 256 41 344381/
349052
Fax: 256 41 254867

ZAMBIA

UNZA Press
PO Box 32379
Lusaka
Tel: 260 1 290409
Fax: 260 1 253952

ZIMBABWE

Weaver Press
PO Box A1922
Avondale
Harare
Tel: 263 4 308330
Fax: 263 4 339645